This book is an extremely practical approach for teaching skills to psychologist helping other parents, I especially appreciate the spec shift the way we react to different types of challenges, changing th teachable moments and opportunities for connection. The format of the book is easy to navigate, and easy to digest. It is a great reference to have for common challenges that emerge for many of our children at home, at school, and out in the great, wide world.

—**Liz Angoff**, PhD, Educational Psychologist and Mom of a preschooler

Although social/emotional learning (SEL) is a complex topic, teaching it need not be a chore or overly challenging. Elizabeth Sautter provides parents with simple, applicable tools to grow and expand skills through activities they're already doing every day – no special preparation or equipment needed.

—**Maureen Bennie**, Director, Autism Awareness Centre and Parent of two adults with autism

Make Social and Emotional Learning Stick! is an engaging and comprehensive book for anyone who teaches or for parents and children. Sautter offers an excellent overview of what social learning involves and then gives readers a gazillion specific ideas to try in a variety of environments. I particularly love the job-talk items for encouraging the child's active involvement and the activity chart makes it easy to relate the activities to specific goal areas.

—**Kari Dunn Buron**, autism education specialist, and author of *When My Worries Get Too Big!* and *Adalyn's Clare*

This valuable resource has blown me out of the water! Elizabeth has taken great care to not only give the "what" but also the "how" to help guide our kids on the journey of social and emotional learning. The activities are short and doable for every family to jump right in to build confident kids!

—**Heather Davis**, Building Confident Kids and mom of a preschooler and middle schooler

This book offers so many ideas that families can use to create teachable moments in everyday life. It's the perfect way to reinforce and practice essential social-emotional skills!

—**Janine Halloran**, LMHC, Founder of Coping Skills for Kids and mom of two middle-school children

"If you could use fresh ideas to support your child's social emotional development (and who couldn't?), you're guaranteed to find some in this extensive compendium of strategies and resources."

—**Julie King**, co-author of *How To Talk So LITTLE Kids Will Listen: A Survival Guide to Life with Children Ages 2-7.*

Elizabeth Sautter has given us a great how-to book on a topic parents want most: how to help socially challenged children feel included and make friends. Activities cover the social situations that confront a child, from first moments of waking to bedtime and from typical days to special event days and holidays. Parents, teachers, and professionals will be able to use the ideas to create a seamless system of support across all settings, teaching the nuts-and-bolts of social behaviors that can lead to social success. I can foresee the book providing great ideas for developing IEP goals. Sautter's latest book is a must-have for professionals and parents alike.

—**Amy Kossow**, parent advocate and mom of son with autism

In a truly visionary fashion, Elizabeth has recognized that executive functioning skills and social skills are both integral to the development of social competence. Additionally, she has recognized that, much like tourists visiting an unknown country, parents of children with social and emotional learning challenges need a guidebook telling them what to watch for. In *Make Social and Emotional Learning Stick!*, she provides this much-needed guidebook to help families incorporate skill building through the day-to-day activities of family life.

—**Carrie Lindemuth**, executive functioning coach, educational therapist,
and parent of two sons, one with autism.

As a school psychologist and mother to two highly sensitive children, I have read countless books on child development and social and emotional learning. There is nothing else on the market with as many practical and tangible tips to help parents make social-emotional learning actually come alive and "stick" across a wide range of day-to-day situations. This book should be in the hands of every parent and every professional who supports families.

—**Katie Raher**, school psychologist, social-emotional trainer, and mom of two sensitive school-age children

Make Social and Emotional Learning Stick! is a helpful guide for parents seeking practical guidance on how to weave SEL into everyday life in a way that's fun and relevant for their children. I especially love that the book is organized so readers can easily access specific ideas and understand exactly how to successfully execute them.

—**Debbie Reber**, author of *Differently Wired*, founder of Tilt Parenting, and mom of a teen

Elizabeth Sautter's approach is music to any parent's ears. In the second edition of *Make Social and Emotional Learning Stick*, parents are reminded to start with wisdom, intentionality, and self-care. And by keeping strategies simple, this practical gem guides you to build confidence for the whole family and reconnect to the joy of parenting.

—**Elaine Taylor-Klaus**, PCC, CPCC, co-founder of ImpactParents.com,
author of *The Essential Guide to Raising Complex Kids*, mom of three complex kids

I highly recommend Elizabeth Sautter's revised edition of *Make Social and Emotional Learning Stick!* Drawing on her personal experiences as well as her broad professional knowledge, this is a wonderful source for parents, teachers, and clinicians. The format is very easy to follow, the activities are clearly described, and the chapter headings make it easy to quickly find what you are looking for. A wonderful addition to your library!

—**Anna Vagin**, PhD, Speech Language Pathologist, author of *Movie Time Social Learning* and *YouCue Feelings*.

Make Social and Emotional Learning Stick! will be welcomed by parents and teachers alike! In easy-to-understand language, Elizabeth Sautter provides over 200 activities that support social and emotional development during daily routines and across various settings, from home to school to community. Readers learn to take advantage of the many natural teaching moments that pop up every day to encourage a child's social-emotional learning.

—**Michelle Garcia Winner**, MA, SLP; founder of the Social Thinking® methodology

MAKE SOCIAL AND EMOTIONAL LEARNING STICK!

Practical activities to help your child manage emotions, navigate social situations & reduce anxiety

Elizabeth A. Sautter, M.A., CCC-SLP

MakeSocialLearningStick.com

Cover design by Debbie O'Byrne at JETLAUNCH
Interior design by JETLAUNCH

Published by Make Social Learning Stick
MakeSocialLearningStick.com

Printed & Distributed by Generation Mindful
GenMindful.com

ISBN: 978-1-64184-476-5 (Paperback)

ISBN: 978-1-64184-428-4 (eBook)

This book is dedicated to my older sister,
Amy, who has navigated the world
with developmental delays.
I'm so proud of your resilience and
achievements over the years.
Thank you for all that
you have taught me and
for inspiring me to help others.

I love you!

Contributors

Rebecca Branstetter, PhD, is a school psychologist, speaker, and author of several books on conscious parenting, ADHD, and executive functioning. She is on a mission to help parents and educators be champions for children to be the best they can be in school and life, and she is the co-collaborator of the Make It Stick online parenting course. She is the founder of The Thriving School Psychologist Collective.™ https://rebeccabranstetter.com

Kari Dunn Buron, MS Ed, is an autism education specialist in Minnesota. She has written several books related to autism, self-management, and emotional regulation, as well as the popular curriculum, *The Incredible 5-Point Scale*. https://www.5pointscale.com

Leah Kuypers, MA Ed, OTR/L, is an occupational therapist and author of *The Zones of Regulation*, a curriculum to foster self-regulation. She provides training internationally on self-regulation and the Zones of Regulation. www.zonesofregulation.com

Kelly Mahler, MS, OTD, OTR/L, is an occupational therapist and adjunct professor at Elizabethtown College who specializes in self-regulation and sensory processing, with a special expertise in interoception. She presents internationally on the eight resources she has authored, including *The Interoception Curriculum*. https://www.kelly-mahler.com

Emily Rubin, MS, CCC-SLP, is the Director of Educational Outreach at Communication Crossroads in Atlanta, GA. She is a co-author of *The SCERTS Assessment Process* and *Social Emotional Engagement–Knowledge and Skills,* and is one of the creators of the SEE-KS model. http://www.commxroads.com

Sarah Ward, MS, CCC-SLP is a speech and language pathologist who specializes in executive function skills. Co-author of the innovative *360 Thinking* executive function program, she travels the world to share this innovative approach and practical strategies for executive functioning. https://efpractice.com

Michelle Garcia Winner, MA, CCC-SLP, is the founder of the *Social Thinking Methodology* and globally recognized as a thought leader, author, speaker, and social-cognitive therapist. She was honored to receive a Congressional Special Recognition Award in 2008. She specializes in concepts to promote the development of executive functions and related social and emotional competencies. https://www.socialthinking.com

Pamela Wolfberg, PhD, is a professor in the Department of Special Education at San Francisco State University, where she coordinates the Autism Spectrum Graduate Certificate program. She is the creator of *Integrated Play Groups®* (*IGP*) and author of several other resources about play and social learning. http://www.wolfberg.com

Ruth Weir Prystash has worked in the field of autism for over forty years as an award-winning teacher, university instructor, presenter, editor, and private consultant. She is a cofounder of the Reach Autism Program in Riverside, California. ruthprystash@gmail.com

Other Books & Products

There are many additional FREE resources, information, and downloads on MakeSocialLearningStick.com to support you. Hop on over and get connected...it takes a village to help you along the way!

***Make SOCIAL Learning Stick!* Card Deck**
***Make EMOTIONAL Learning Stick!* Card Deck**

Anytime ideas for busy parents on the go to help you boost your child's emotional intelligence, manage emotions and navigate social situations.

• • •

Whole Body Listening Larry at Home
and
Whole Body Listening Larry at School
(with Kristen Wilson)

Children's books to teach how to listen with your whole body

• • •

Zones of Regulation Products:

Zones Storybooks
Tools to Try Card Decks - One for kids, one for teens
(with Leah Kuypers)
Navigating the Zones Game
(with Leah Kuypers and Terri Rossman)

Make it Stick Parenting Course and Community
Online course and support for parents

MakeSocialLearningstick.com

Contents

Contents

Foreword

It is rare to meet someone so like-minded as Elizabeth Sautter. Within minutes of meeting her, I knew she was a kindred spirit, another professional impassioned to serve individuals with social and emotional learning challenges, and vested in educating and equipping others on how to better support these individuals. That was a decade ago. I was in the process of moving across the country while working on the publication of my soon-be-released book, *The Zones of Regulation* (2011). I was struggling to find meaningful employment where I would be able to put my expertise in building regulation and social cognitive skills into practice, while also working alongside other professionals who valued these skills. I was beginning to question if I could find such a match, but that all changed when I found Elizabeth's name on a list of professionals who had completed the Social Thinking® (socialthinking.com) mentorship program run by Michelle Garcia-Winner.

As a follower of the Social Thinking methodology, I had reached out to other Social Thinking-trained professionals listed in the Bay Area, and Elizabeth Sautter responded. Elizabeth, co-owner of Communication Works (cwtherapy.com), a practice comprised of speech and language pathologists serving clients in the Bay Area, had no intention of bringing an occupational therapist into the practice. However, she had a hunch that I might be worth considering. When I informed her that I would be in the area looking at jobs, she jumped on the chance to meet me in person. I came to our dinner meeting with my draft of *The Zones of Regulation,* and she devoured it, leading to discussions of how my work could complement the services being offered by Communication Works. Before I knew it, I had a job offer, as well as a soul sister who I could talk to (and geek out with) for hours on all things related to our favorite topics: self-regulation, social cognition, and executive functioning.

As Elizabeth and I worked together at her clinic, Elizabeth's creativity was abundantly clear. She has an unbelievable capacity to absorb knowledge in our field, a true maven. However, what sets her apart is her unique ability to take that knowledge and apply it meaningfully, not just for those on her caseload, but also for their caregivers. Her impact has been incredibly powerful because she has equipped caregivers with practical information and skills to better support children, not just at school, but through the ins-and-outs of everyday living. Elizabeth's drive to support the caregivers and families of the children she serves is personal. She grew up with an older sister with special needs, and has a nephew on the autism spectrum, as well as a son with unique learning needs. Elizabeth's firsthand experience in living with and supporting a person with a disability drove her to find solutions to better prepare caregivers in delivering social emotional learning supports to children in the little moments in daily living. Before long, Elizabeth was pumping out books and supports to help with her mission, including *Whole Body Listening Larry at Home* and *School*, as well as the first edition of *Make Social Learning Stick*. The passion that brought Elizabeth and I together a decade ago continues to bind us together as therapists, colleagues, friends, and authors. We have collaborated on companion products to the *Zones of Regulation®* curriculum, including *Navigating The Zones* and the *Zones of Regulation* Storybooks and Tool cards. Elizabeth is also a collaborative speaker, presenting on *The Zones* to groups around the country.

Make Social Learning Stick provides an easy-to-use graphic guide for caregivers to support social emotional learning in the everyday life of a child. As a therapist myself, the challenge we often face is how to take the work we do with a child in the often short time we have together to carry over into the child's real-world living. The more we can build the capacity of caregivers to find and coach children during daily teachable moments, the more likely the children will be to take the skills that are being addressed in therapeutic settings/classrooms and demonstrate them in real time in the home, community, and school. Elizabeth saw the need to provide caregivers with easily accessible resources to support these vital social emotional skills, and she created *Make Social Learning Stick* to specifically meet that need.

Given the positive feedback she received from *Make Social Learning Stick's* first edition, it is no surprise that Elizabeth has expanded upon the original book to include even more ideas and content in this updated second edition. In true Elizabeth fashion, Elizabeth doesn't stop there. She goes above and beyond with this book by also including contributions from numerous experts in the field, weaving together how different strategies can be used in conjunction with one another. For example, *Make Social Learning Stick* includes a visual with instructions on my *Zones of Regulation* tool, the Six Sides of Breathing; Kelly Mahler's work in interoception; Sarah Ward's work in executive functioning; Michelle Garcia Winner's concepts of Social Thinking, and much more. Elizabeth is a true collaborator in the field, and this book certainly reflects that collaborative spirit.

As I travel around the world, training on the *Zones of Regulation*, I hear from concerned people that today's children are a much needier population than those of the past. While I don't have the answer for why today's youth have higher needs in social and emotional learning, I am proud to contribute to the resources that address this need with my own work. In the arena of social emotional learning, it is exciting to see the expansion of resources that support children in the acquisition of vital lifetime skills. However, with many titles in this area geared for therapists or teachers, there is a huge gap in what is being offered for the caregiver. Elizabeth Sautter's 2nd edition with the new title of *Make Social and Emotional Learning Stick* is the exception, filling this void with tangible, easy-to-use guidance for caregivers. For any parent or caregiver wondering what they can do to help foster their child's social and emotional skills, this book is for you. If you've pondered what you can do to help your child be more resilient and better handle the bumps in the road, this book is for you. For the grandparents hoping to help your grandchildren be prepared and take on the responsibilities that come with growing up, this book is for you. It is an honor to have Elizabeth as a friend and colleague, and it is an honor to present to you her incredible work, *Make Social and Emotional Learning Stick, 2nd Edition.*

Leah Kuypers, MA Ed, OTR/L

Preface

Since writing the first edition of *Make Social Learning Stick!* in 2014, my own skills and expertise have evolved, both through my professional work and from raising my two sons. I've been diving into the explosion of brain-based research about fostering social and emotional learning and child development. I'm eager to share this fascinating and exciting new information, including practical strategies for incorporating it in a format that remains easy to grasp and use. The intent is not to create extra work for parents and caregivers, but rather to offer activities and ideas that can easily be incorporated into daily routines to support the whole child. These strategies are not "add-ons" to your busy caregiving and parenting life, but "add-*ins*" to reinforce social learning in your daily routines.

I have learned however, that strategies can't stand alone; they need a supportive system to make them effective. Let me explain a bit more. As a therapist and coach, I have always searched for the latest-and-greatest new strategy with my clients and my own children. In the past, this sent me down a rabbit hole of Google searches, scrambling to review my sticky notes from all of the research, therapy resources, and parenting books I had read. When I tried something new, my children would sometimes resist and complain, especially as they got older. I then replied with something crazy like, "Research shows this will help X, Y, or Z!" I felt like a strategy saleswoman, and they were slamming the door in my face.

Something was missing, but I didn't know what. I eventually found a workshop on mindfulness that sounded intriguing, and that ultimately changed my life. After weeks of training and practice, a lightbulb went off around my challenges with "selling" strategies. It became clear to me that implementing strategies alone was not enough.

I realized that the foundation that best supports children, families, and educators includes three key components that precede the implementation of a strategy: wisdom, intentionality, and self-care. In my own home, if these pillars are not solid, I find that strategies are less effective and are often rejected. From this "aha" moment, the WISE model was born (described later in this book).

I have been practicing mindfulness for over five years now. I strive to be conscious and intentional in my daily parenting and to focus on realistic goals. Admittedly, there are moments when all the knowledge I have about best practices in parenting do not work because I skip right to a "default strategy," which usually happens when I am neglecting my own self-care or am not connected with my children or myself. This is why self-care is a key ingredient. It gives us the strength and patience for the millions of parenting decisions we must make on the fly. It is this strength and patience that allows us to be the best possible social coaches for our children. Mindfulness was one of the motivations for updating this book, as it is the foundation for all of the other strategies.

This second edition, with the updated title of *Make Social and Emotional Learning Stick*, is divided into three parts. In Part One, I included an extended introduction with an overview and definitions. Part Two includes all of the suggested activities. Part Three provides additional learning strategies. In this updated edition, I added the following features to make the book even more helpful for parents and caregivers:

- The WISE model (from the *Make It Stick Parenting* online course, at GenMindful.com), a system to support parents and caregivers as they try new strategies so they can move from on-the-fly parenting to strategic and proactive parenting.
- More strategies from additional leading experts and colleagues in the field.

- New activities for home and community.
- An entirely new section of activities focused on building the home/school connection.
- Additional resources and parent-friendly definitions that cut through the jargon, so you have a clearer understanding of the terms that school staff and professionals may use to describe your child's challenges and to help you to understand your child's strengths and areas of challenge.
- Supplementary activity card decks (sold separately) to provide an easy, portable format for on-the-go strategies.

The tools and strategies I offer here are primarily targeted toward children with additional needs in the areas of social, emotional, and executive functioning. However, they may also be helpful for children who may just need a little extra support with social behavior or peer interaction in general. Hopefully, these ideas and tools will provide a layer of strategies and activities that can be applied in everyday life to ultimately help support the development of the whole child.

My goal with this second edition is to provide simple suggestions to build confidence for both parents and children, offering a stress-free option for embracing these natural learning opportunities with joy and ease. Parenting is not easy! And there is no handbook or training that we get before we embark on the journey. My hope is that this book will provide tips, strategies, and ideas that give you the tools you need to make the journey a little easier by gaining the confidence to embrace each moment as a teachable one to build social and emotional learning.

Elizabeth

PART ONE
INTRODUCTION

A Daily Struggle

It's time for Johnny to get up and get ready for school. He hears his dad calling him for the third time to get up, get ready, and come eat breakfast so he isn't late for school again. His body feels sluggish, he doesn't want to wear any of the clothes that are clean, and he didn't practice his spelling words. *I'm sure I'll do badly on my test!* he thinks to himself and remembers that there is also a school assembly that day. *It's so loud in the auditorium! Who will I sit next to?* he wonders silently, as the sounds of his sister's singing reaches his ears, annoying him even further. "I hate school!" he yells, loudly enough for his dad to hear him.

His dad comes in to talk with Johnny, and Johnny tells him that he doesn't understand why he can't remember to study for quizzes or turn in his assignments. Johnny also says that he has been trying to join in when the other kids are talking about movies or video games, but he always seems to say the wrong thing. And when he approaches the kids playing tag at recess, they always tell him he has to be "it," and that's no fun. He has been sitting on the bench at recess, reading and pretending he doesn't care, even though he is feeling rejected by his peers and confused about what to do.

Johnny's parents and teachers have been concerned and wonder if he is being teased. He has been struggling in school, often sits alone at lunchtime, and rarely gets invited to birthday parties or social events outside of school. Some mornings he tells his parents he is too sick to go to school. His parents, grandparents, and babysitter all see how lonely Johnny is but don't know how to help.

How Can We Help Johnny?

Our world is filled with sticky situations that we navigate by knowing what to say, how to act, or what is appropriate for each situation. This can be a struggle for those who are not hard-wired to pick up on social cues, have trouble managing their emotions, or struggle to understand how their behavior affects other people.

Challenges in these areas can have a negative impact on a child's mental health and quality of life, causing pain and worry for those affected and for the people who love them. Both Johnny and his family are negatively affected by his lack of social success. However, the good news is that essential skills can be taught, practiced, and improved. And we—parents, caregivers and educators—can help!

What concrete steps can Johnny's parents and caregivers take to help him with his daily struggles at home and school? *Make Social and Emotional Learning Stick!* answers that question. Using a menu of hands-on activities through everyday routines like mealtimes, getting ready for school, and shopping for groceries, we can utilize common life situations and events as opportunities to embrace teachable moments that help build and practice skills in a natural setting. The activities and suggestions presented in the book teach essential life skills for children like Johnny who often struggle with social learning. These include:

- Think about others
- Be flexible
- Follow directions
- Read social cues
- Work in small groups
- Participate in conversations
- Advocate for oneself
- See the big picture
- Plan ahead
- Develop empathy
- Make friends

Research shows that the brain has the ability to change, build stronger pathways, and grow connections. We can exercise our brain with activities like the ones described in this book, to develop social, emotional, and executive functioning skills, just as we work out at the gym to gain flexibility and develop stronger muscles. By doing these activities, we teach a very important set of skills. These crucial skills are known as Social Emotional Learning.

Social Emotional Learning: A Deeper Look

Social Emotional Learning (SEL) is the process by which children and adults learn to build relationships, identify and manage their own emotions, learn empathy and how to take the perspective of others, and how to make good choices in their daily lives. The importance of these skills cannot be overstated; they play a major role in developing and maintaining relationships, as well as in academic achievement, the ability to work in small groups, and the opportunity to eventually hold a job (Blair, 2002; Bodrova & Leong, 2005).

Over the years, leading experts and researchers have been working hard to build awareness about the importance of SEL and to make it clear that these skills are the foundation for academic and life success. It is exciting to see curricula developed and implemented in many classrooms and schools for all children, not just those who are delayed in these areas. One organization, the Collaborative for Academic, Social, and Emotional Learning (CASEL), has identified five basic Social Emotional Learning Competencies. These include: self-awareness, self-management, social awareness, relationship skills, and responsible decision-making. These are skills that all children require and who most acquire as a typical part of their development.

However, children like Johnny require extra support to attain these skills. Many of the students within the special education system, and some who don't have designated extra support, will require additional assistance to learn and practice the five competencies.

Social and emotional learning be especially difficult for individuals with extra challenges such as anxiety, attention deficits, or social and behavioral challenges. If a child struggles to focus, think about others, or manage emotions, it is hard to think about the external environment—the people around us and the skills needed to relate to them. This is why it is critical to take a deeper look at what is involved with these skills prior to diving in to help.

SEL skills are governed by a set of mental processes: self-regulation, which includes sensory processing; emotional regulation and executive functioning; and social communication, which includes joint attention, receptive and expressive language, pragmatic language, and perspective taking.

Self-regulation is the ability to gain control of bodily functions, manage powerful emotions, and maintain focus and attention (Shonkoff & Phillips, 2000). This is similar to self-control, self-management, anger management, and impulse control. The three main components of self-regulation, with which many of our children struggle, are *sensory processing, emotional regulation, and executive functioning.*

- **Sensory processing** is the way we receive and manage information from the environment through our senses (Ayres, 2005). We actually have eight senses: sight, smell, hearing, touch, taste, proprioception (the ability to feel our body even if we can't see it), vestibular (movement and balance), and interoception (awareness of internal sensations, such as hunger or sleepiness). When children have sensory systems that are over or under-reactive, it can be difficult for them to process sensory input and feel comfortable internally, which affects their behavior.
- **Emotional regulation** refers to the ability to control our emotions rather than letting them control us. Everyone experiences emotions, but we can regulate the timing, display, duration, and intensity of how our emotions are expressed or revealed depending on the social situation. On the other hand, when our emotions control us, we might act before thinking and do something that gets us in trouble or makes someone else upset.
- **Executive functioning** is the cognitive process required to plan and direct activities (Dawson & Guare, 2010). It involves skills for emotional and impulse control, attention, motivation, flexibility, problem solving, planning, organization, and initiating. Executive function skills allow us to manage the emotions we experience as well as monitor our behavior and ability to have effective communicative exchanges. It also involves the ability to integrate *future* anticipation (forethought) with *past* experience (hindsight) to develop a reasonable plan for a *present* action or goal (Ward & Jacobsen, 2012). Being able to stay calm—as well as plan, organize, and initiate goals based on hindsight and forethought—are all part of executive functioning.

Social communication is defined by the American Speech and Hearing Association (ASHA) as the use of language in social contexts. It involves *joint attention, receptive and expressive language, pragmatic language, and perspective taking.*

- **Joint attention** is being able to share attention with another person and is achieved when one person alerts another person to an object, situation/event, or person by using a gesture (e.g., pointing) or eye gaze. When the individual's awareness is brought to a similar object/situation by another person, they can then share focus and engage in conversation, play, or shared thoughts.
- **Receptive language** is the ability to process and understand language and to follow directions. It helps us gain information and understand information from sounds, words, gestures, and writing/visual information, as well as from routines and watching others (e.g., knowing that it's time to go to recess when reading is over and others are lining up).
- **Expressive language** involves communication using verbal, nonverbal, and written modes of communication (sounds, words, sentences, gestures, sign language, technology, written language, etc.). It involves the ability to label and describe objects, put words together into sentences using correct grammar, tell and write stories, and answer questions.
- **Pragmatic or social language** refers to the ability to understand the words being spoken and messages being sent, as well as the context (e.g., culture or situation), in order to know what, when, and how to effectively communicate with others. This enables us to alter our communication to adapt to the situation at hand. It also includes our tone of voice, facial expressions, body posture, hand gestures, proximity, and other nonverbal clues.
- **Perspective taking** is the important ability to "step into someone's shoes" or take another person's perspective (Baron-Cohen, Leslie, & Frith, 1985). It allows us to think about other people and what they might be thinking about or feeling and to understand that their thoughts, feelings, desires, and experiences differ from our own.

As you can see, SEL is extremely complex, especially for those who need more support with the components listed above. Over the years, I have offered the term "social regulation" (Sautter and Kuypers, 2012) as a way to conceptualize everything involved with self-regulation and social communication and how they are interconnected. We define **social regulation** as the ability to adjust our level of alertness and modify how we reveal emotions and behavior in order to achieve social goals. In other words, it is the ability to monitor and adjust internal feelings and states (both mental and physical) in order to exhibit behavior that is expected for a social situation. This definition is not meant to replace SEL. However, it does provide a deeper meaning and explanation for what is involved to those who might not pick up the skills through traditional development and teaching.

Supporting Children with Compassion

All of the areas defined above are developmental in nature. The skills develop over time, just like walking and talking, but when there are delays, challenging behaviors often occur. We might see children who struggle with academics, forget to raise their hand before talking, yell when upset, or shut down when overwhelmed. They might struggle to work in groups or make friends. These children are often labeled as a behavioral problem, challenged, loner, drama queen, or unmotivated, to name a few. In reality, they are struggling to meet the demands of the moment, which are often too difficult for their abilities or skills. They are not *giving* us a hard time; they are *having* a hard time!

Behavior is communication, and the challenging behavior that we see on the outside is an indication that they need more help. The overt behavior is like the tip of the iceberg: It's our job to lower the water line to determine what support is needed. These kids need to be met with compassion and understanding to determine where they have delayed skills; they need extra teaching, scaffolding, and practice. Dr. Ross Greene sums it up perfectly, "Kids do well if they ***can***!" When they are not doing well, it is our job to figure out why and to discover where their skill development is lagging, to support them and meet their needs. With this compassionate view in mind, and by understanding the complexity and depth of SEL, parents and teachers can jump in to provide the needed support.

Parent-Teacher Partnerships Support the Whole Child

The book's new activity section on school offers strategies for parents and caregivers to develop productive partnerships with educators to enhance the team approach. The schoolday provides frequent opportunities to reinforce social, emotional, and executive functioning skills. Many teachers incorporate social-emotional activities in their classrooms, ranging from social-emotional skills in the curriculum to using these skills as teachable moments throughout the day. These activities and strategies can benefit the child at home, just as what parents and caregivers do at home can support the child at school. The suggestions in this book are designed to develop a parent-teacher partnership that serves the child's specific needs. It's helpful for parents to visualize their child's life at school to prepare the child for success while also supporting the educators.

It can be challenging to fully support a child when home and school are compartmentalized, so having information flow back and forth can provide the best of both worlds by building consistency. Ideally, the home and school teams collaborate and share resources. When a partnership between home and school exists, this facilitates and enforces the acquisition of skills and increases the likelihood that a positive behavior change is maintained over time (Koegel, Matos-Fredeen, Lang, & Koegel, 2011). All adults in a child's life are educators of sorts, with parents usually providing the greatest influence and strongest models. Building a bridge between home and school is, however, how adults can best support and strengthen the whole child. By building consistency between home and school, everyone wins!

Parents Need Tools and Strategies Too!

Just as "kids do well if they can," so do parents and caregivers. And just as children need strategies to develop certain skills, adults need strategies to teach these complex skills. This book is designed to do just that—to be a resource for strategies and ideas that will give you confidence to support your child's SEL skills.

Teaching SEL can't be confined only to therapy sessions or school. It has to take place in the child's natural environment—something I know well through my experience as a therapist who believes in a family-centered approach and as a family member and parent of those who have lagging skills in these areas. This kind of support happens seven days a week and needs to be infused into all aspects of the child's life and daily schedule, not only with their friends or at school, but also at home and in other settings. Social and emotional learning happens everywhere, every day, all day. In order to support a child's ability to be successful in a variety of environments, it is important to realize that social situations and expectations may change rapidly or fluidly throughout your child's day. Therefore, the objective is for your child to have the skills necessary to be adaptable so that they can be successful in a variety of these environments.

While this sounds like a tall order when added to everything else you need to do, it can easily become part of your daily schedule without too much fuss or added stress, using the tools and strategies illustrated in this book. Including parents, caregivers, and other family members as social facilitators is essential to a child's success. *This is the glue that makes the skills stick!*

The WISE Model

The **WISE** model was developed to support the process of building these skills and parenting in general. It is also part of the *Make It Stick Parenting* online training program developed by Dr. Rebecca Branstetter and me. **WISE** stands for **W**isdom, **I**ntentionality, **S**elf-care, and **E**veryday Strategies. These four pillars are the foundation for the activities in this new edition of the book. I invite you to also visit the MakeSocialLearningStick.com website and learn more about the course and the community we created. Here is a brief overview of the components of the WISE model:

W—Wisdom

The W in the WISE model stands for **wisdom**. We need to be aware and mindful of what is going on around us to tap into knowledge we have or might need to gain to help ourselves, our children, and our families. This might seem simple, but it's not as easy as it sounds.

We become more aware through mindfulness practices. Mindfulness can help us pause and pay attention with intention, without judging yourself or the situation. A lot of evidence shows that mindfulness can help us observe and become more aware of our thoughts and feelings and to consciously respond to our children's ever-changing emotions, behaviors, and needs (Weare, 2002). Mindfulness helps us become less critical of ourselves and our children and stay grounded, even when others (including our children) are not. It creates the pause we need to think clearly with intent and compassion for others and ourselves. When we can achieve this, we can become curious about our child's behavior, skills, and needs, and seek help when needed.

Mindfulness can be practiced through breathing exercises, yoga, mindful listening, mindful eating, and compassion practices. Online classes, books, and apps can help you get started or support existing mindfulness practices. And don't worry if the traditional type of mindfulness and meditation isn't your thing; you don't have to sit for an hour in a silent meditation retreat to be mindful. Maybe you can take baby steps. Put your phone down while you eat to focus on each bite, savor your morning cup of coffee by noticing the aroma and warming your hands while holding the mug with gratitude, or snuggle with your child and notice the smell of their hair. Try to notice a specific moment in time and the sensations you are feeling. Even notice when you are not in the moment—that is mindfulness, too. Just be sure to leave the judgment behind and not beat yourself up, even though it can be hard, especially in a hectic world.

Mindfulness is equally important for adults and children alike. It can be the missing piece of the puzzle that helps increase emotional and social awareness. Start with yourself and learn with your child through the suggestions provided throughout this book and the optional supplementary cards.

I—Intentionality

Becoming grounded, aware, and wise through mindfulness can help you to pause, think rationally, and be **intentional** about what your child needs in any given moment. When you increase your awareness and focus, you can develop a clear plan for addressing your child's lagging skills. Without an intentional plan, you might fall back on whatever is easiest at that time, rather than harnessing a teachable moment. Think about what you are trying to teach your child and how you can model the values and lessons you want them to learn. Intentionality helps parents and caregivers focus on these important questions:

- What matters most in that moment and in the future?
- What needs or lagging skills should I focus on in the current moment?
- How can I be conscious of my child's needs without neglecting my own?

After setting intentions and implementing them in realtime, reflect and revise as needed. Being intentional includes asking yourself, "How did that go?" and "What could I do differently next time?" As you try new strategies with your child, I recommend taking these steps:

a) Set your intentions based on your child's needs and goals.
b) Implement a new activity or strategy based on these intentions.
c) Reflect on how things went and what could be improved.

We all have good intentions. In stressful, emotionally charged, or high-pressure situations, we frequently go into "default mode." This can often exacerbate the situation and make it worse or at least be a missed opportunity to teach our kids the very critical missing skills that are likely creating the challenge in the first place. And we also miss the chance to reflect on ourselves and learn how to better handle similar situations in the future.

S—Self-Care

As parents and caregivers, our day-to-day lives can be stressful and often focus on meeting the needs of other people before ourselves. There's a good reason for the statement, "Put on your own oxygen mask before assisting others." Without your own oxygen, you lose the ability to help anyone else. Likewise, if you think about yourself as a pitcher of water whose job is to fill the glasses (children) around you, it's vital that your pitcher has enough water to pour. It is not selfish to care for yourself—it's a necessity.

To establish a self-care routine, take the time to create and implement a plan to meet your own needs. Back to the water pitcher analogy, self-care goes beyond drinking enough liquids each day; it is also eating healthy foods and getting enough exercise. Physical care and biological needs are important, but also consider emotional, spiritual, social/relationships, and work/life balance. Do you have a good support system in place? Do you have time to recharge and do the things that fill your bucket? It can be helpful to map out what is working and not working and try to include more tools for yourself (e.g., mindfulness, walking, taking time to enjoy your coffee or tea in a quiet space, making sure your kids go to sleep at a time that allows you some down time, getting out in nature, connecting with friends, etc.).

In addition, children learn by watching the adults around them and how they take care of themselves and regulate their own emotional needs. While you are doing this, don't forget to talk to your kids about what you are doing (e.g., "I'm starting to feel frustrated, so I'm going to go in my room and do some breathing" or "Wow, it feels good to go for a walk before I start my day").

In the rush of everyday life, it's easy to ignore self-care. Some parents even tell me they feel guilty for taking "me" time. Just know that when you fill your self-care pitcher, you will be better at handling stressful parenting moments, and you will also be modeling a critical life skill for your child. It's a two-for-one!

E-Everyday Strategies

The tools, ideas, and strategies for everyday use offered in this book provide many simple ways that you can embed teachable moments to build SEL into natural life situations. Before layering on these strategies, it's important to put in place the pillars of wisdom, intentionality, and self-care. These pillars will enable you to thoughtfully choose and implement the strategies that make the most sense for your child and to select the right times for using them.

Using the WISE model will help you get the most benefit from the strategies offered in this book, as it gives you information on what to try with your child, as well as how to be a more effective social coach.

Some of these strategies will fit your child's needs and others may not. For this reason, I've included more than 200 activities for parents and teachers to consider. Abraham Maslow said, "If the only tool you have is a hammer, you tend to see every problem as a nail." So select strategies with care and intention, and don't be discouraged if you have to try different approaches before finding the best fit. My hope is that these strategies will be helpful, and they will also inspire you to create and test some of your own. As a parent, caregiver, or educator, you're already using a variety of strategies (consciously or unconsciously) to help your children. Trust and have confidence in the fact that you are playing a vital role in making your child's skills stick.

How the Book Is Organized

Part One provides concepts and definitions for Social Emotional Learning (SEL) and introduces the information covered throughout the book. Part Two is divided into four major sections of practical activities: (a) At Home, (b) In the Community, (c) Holidays and Special Events and, (d) Bridging Home and School. Each section focuses on daily routines and activities and gives suggestions for increasing participation and skill development within those situations. Part Two is not meant to be read straight through, and the activities aren't meant to be used in a particular order. However, information is presented in sequential order according to the flow of the day to help with organization. Within each section, strategies are grouped by daily, weekly, and yearly activities and according to events that occur in most families' lives. Part Three includes fourteen extra learning strategies with further information on how to boost the power of the activities and efforts around building SEL in all environments.

Each activity in Part Two includes **hidden rules**, the unstated rules in various social settings, also referred to as social rules. For those who don't learn social norms intuitively, the hidden rules, or hidden curriculum

(Myles, Trautman, & Schelvan, 2013), can be extremely abstract, confusing, and continuously changing. The hidden rules need to be explained and reinforced on a regular basis. For example, we might think a child knows that taking food from another person's plate or taking up too much space on an airplane seat is considered rude, but some children are unaware of these unstated rules. When we engage our children with activities such as those in this book, we also need to direct their attention to the hidden rules and specifics of each situation. We can prepare them in advance by reviewing the rules or setting, checking in during the activity, and debriefing afterward. In this way, our job as coaches expands even more as we must teach our children to look around them and then guide them in interpreting what they see. Initially, it may be exhausting to think about the world in this way, but it will eventually become second nature for both you and your child. Take the time to review the applicable social rules and remember to share them with your child either before (preferably), during, or after a social situation. The examples that I provide can be used as a starting point to discuss these various social situations and the rules that go along with them to build awareness and understanding.

The book also includes examples of an effective tool called **job talk** (Jacobsen and Ward, 2012). This refers to tasks or actions (verbs) that are turned into nouns. Simply adding "er" to a verb or making the action into an occupation helps the child take ownership and become more willing to jump in and complete the task. For example, instead of saying to the child, "Please help me sweep," try saying, "Can you be the sweeper?" Instead of saying, "Take a picture of that view," say, "You be the photographer." The examples are intended to serve as reminders to use this tool to help the child take ownership and increase motivation to do certain tasks. Job talk can be presented in the form of a question or a request. Give it a try; it's amazing how a small change in language can change a person's attitude!

Throughout the activities you will find user-friendly social learning vocabulary in italics. Many of the terms are part of the Social Thinking Vocabulary developed by Michelle Garcia Winner. They provide a common language that adults can use with children to describe the abstract concepts that are part of everyday social situations—concepts that can be difficult to explain. For example, we can say, "Keep your brain in the group," when a child is daydreaming. This helps the child understand that they need to think about the subject at hand. It is more descriptive, and therefore more concrete, than saying, "stop daydreaming" or "pay attention."

Although this book is targeted toward children who have challenges or delays in specific areas, **the activities presented can enhance skill development for *all* children**. This book provides the how-to explanations—what to do in the moment and how to make that moment teachable. The over-200 fun and easy activities include contributions from leading experts, and I've provided evidence-based strategies and activities that have worked for my family and countless others. The activities are geared toward children from preschool-age and up and can be easily adapted to the child's developmental age, skills, or needs. Use, modify, or change the suggestions as you like. If some activities do not work for your child or family, move on to others that are useful. Select what you need, when you need it, and adapt the activities as you see fit.

These activities will also spark new ideas that you can use and even share with others. Consider keeping this book and the supplementary card decks in a place that is easily accessible to family members and caregivers so that they will remember to review and use the ideas throughout the day. As you incorporate the activities into everyday life, your child will gradually build their skills and become comfortable with those skills in a broad range of situations.

Finally, remember that learning is a process that takes time and patience on the part of children and the adults who support them. Stay with it and try not to be discouraged if some strategies don't work. Most of all, be sure to celebrate your child's efforts and growth and your own essential role in making these skills stick.

Chart of All Activities with Target Areas

**Target Areas (See more in-depth definitions within the introduction)*

- *Sensory Processing (processing sensations-**SP**)*
- *Emotional Regulation (managing emotions-**ER**)*
- *Executive Functioning (managing goals-**EF**)*
- *Joint Attention-(looking together-**JA**)*
- *Receptive Language-(understanding language-**RL**)*
- *Expressive Language (communicating-**EL**)*
- *Pragmatic Language (social rules-**PL**)*
- *Perspective Taking (thinking of others-**PT**)*

AT HOME

	Page	SP	ER	EF	JA	RL	EL	PL	PT
START THE DAY									
My Morning Schedule	*20*		X	X		X			
Backup Plan	*20*		X	X					
Intention of the Day	*20*		X	X					
Time to Wake Up	*21*	X	X	X					
Body Check-In	*21*	X	X	X					
Weather Detective	*21*	X	X	X					
RULES FOR HAVING FUN									
Review the Rules	*22*		X		X	X		X	X
Adding to the Fun	*22*		X		X	X		X	X
Fair Play	*22*		X		X				X
ENCOURAGE PLAY WITH PEERS AND SIBLINGS									
Special Space	*23*	X	X	X				X	X
Special Time With Peers	*23*			X	X			X	X
Play Routines	*23*		X	X	X	X		X	X
Have Fun!	*23*				X			X	X
PRETEND PLAY									
Dress-Up	*24*		X	X	X			X	X
Building a Fort	*24*				X		X	X	X
Pretend Play: Boxes, Boxes, and More Boxes	*24*		X		X		X		X
Role-Play	*24*		X				X	X	X
INDOOR ANTI-BOREDOM									
No Voice Needed	*25*				X	X		X	X
Treasure Hunt	*25*			X		X			
Would You Rather?	*25*						X		X
CHORES									
Vacuuming	*26*			X	X			X	
Chore Detective	*26*			X	X	X			
Whose Clothes?	*26*			X					X
Clear Vision for a Clean Future	*27*			X		X			
Where Does It Belong?	*27*			X		X			
Partner Chores	*27*		X	X	X				
FURRY FRIENDS									
Animals Help Cope With Emotions	*28*	X	X						
Pets: Help Them, Help Us!	*28*			X				X	X
New Tricks	*28*				X			X	X
Emotional Benefits	*28*		X					X	X
PHONE ETIQUETTE									
Receiving a Call	*29*					X	X	X	X
Don't Be an *Interruptosaurus*!	*29*					X		X	X
Talking on the Phone	*29*			X			X	X	
Hand Signals	*29*				X	X		X	

**Target Areas (See more in-depth definitions within the introduction)*

- *Sensory Processing*-**SP**
- *Emotional Regulation*-**ER**
- *Executive Functioning*-**EF**
- *Joint Attention*-**JA**
- *Receptive Language*-**RL**
- *Expressive Language*-**EL**
- *Pragmatic Language*-**PL**
- *Perspective Taking*-**PT**

AT HOME

	Page	SP	ER	EF	JA	RL	EL	PL	PT
SHOWTIME									
Be a Family Detective	30						X	X	X
I See What You're Thinking	30		X					X	X
Who Gets to Pick?	30		X					X	X
Learning the Characters	30							X	X
FAMILY TOGETHER TIME									
A Picture Is Worth a Thousand Words	31		X		X			X	X
Thinking About the Family	31		X	X			X		X
Family Tree	31						X		X
I Think I'm Thinking!	31		X	X				X	X
TALENT WANTED									
Comic Relief	32		X	X	X		X	X	
Family Skits	32			X	X	X		X	X
Start a Band	32				X	X		X	
Best in Show	32					X		X	
ARTS AND CRAFTS									
Handmade Thoughts	34			X			X	X	X
Drawing Conclusions	34			X				X	
Inside Others' Minds	34					X		X	X
Visualizing with the End in Mind	35			X		X			
Drawing a Snapshot of a Child's Point of View	35					X		X	X
Pretend Pen Pals	35			X			X		X
IN THE KITCHEN									
Service with a Smile	36			X		X	X		X
Surprise Snack	36		X		X	X	X		X
Our Eyes Show Our Thoughts	36				X			X	X
DINNER OR MEAL PREPARATION									
Making Dinner Together	37			X		X			
Food for Thought: What's for Dinner?	37				X	X		X	
Formal Dinners	37		X	X		X		X	
Get Ready, Do, Done!	37			X		X			
AT THE TABLE									
Talking Stick	38		X			X	X		
Conversation Cards	38						X	X	
Dinner Schedule	38			X		X		X	
Listening with the Whole Body	38	X	X		X	X		X	X
Table Guidelines	39			X				X	X
Wonder Questions	39			X			X	X	
"Eye See You"	39				X	X		X	X
NIGHTTIME ROUTINE									
How Was Your Day?	40		X				X		
Nighttime Check-in	40		X	X					
Gratitude	40		X				X		
Sweet Dreams	40		X				X		
Body Scan	41	X	X						
Belly Breathing	41	X	X						
Boxing Up Your Worries	41		X	X			X		

**Target Areas (See more in-depth definitions within the introduction)*

- *Sensory Processing-***SP**
- *Emotional Regulation-***ER**
- *Executive Functioning-***EF**
- *Joint Attention-***JA**
- *Receptive Language-***RL**
- *Expressive Language-***EL**
- *Pragmatic Language-***PL**
- *Perspective Taking-***PT**

AT HOME

	Page	SP	ER	EF	JA	RL	EL	PL	PT
IN THE BATHROOM									
Scrubbing is Loving	42	X		X					X
Following the Steps	42			X		X			
Make a Splash	42	X			X			X	
Mindful Toothbrushing	42	X	X						
READING AND STORY TIME									
Stepping Into the Character's Shoes	44		X		X			X	X
Wordless Picture Books	44		X		X		X	X	X
Reading and Literacy	44		X	X	X				X
Guessing What the Book Is About	44				X			X	X
Tone of Voice	45		X		X		X	X	X
What Would You Do?	45		X	X	X				X
Book Club	45						X		X
The Best Listeners	45		X						X
SEND THOUGHTFUL LETTERS									
Get-Well Wishes	46		X				X		X
Letter of Apology	46		X	X			X		X
Stay in Touch	46		X				X		X
Global Thinker	46		X				X		X
FAMILY CONNECTIONS									
Family Meetings	47		X	X			X		X
Box of Kindness	47		X						X
Play Together to Stay Together	47		X	X	X	X			X
CALM CASA									
Calming Corner	48	X	X						
Spa Day	48	X	X						
Family Yoga	48	X	X						
Basic Needs for Success	48	X	X	X					
SIBLINGS									
What Do We Have in Common?	50		X				X		X
What's Their Side?	50		X	X	X		X		X
Slumber Party	50		X		X				X
Swapping Responsibilities	51			X					X
Star of the Day	51		X						X
Yours, Mine, or Ours?	51		X	X				X	X
Rebooting	51		X	X					X
SCREEN TIME AND MEDIA MANIA									
Where and When?	52		X	X					
Be a Media Model	52		X		X				
Media Vacations	52		X	X					
Teach Me How to Play	52		X		X				X
DAILY TRANSITIONS									
One Step at a Time (First…Then)	53		X	X		X			
Toolbox of Calming Strategies	53	X	X	X					
Transition Songs	53		X	X		X			
Social Rules Change from Situation to Situation	53		X	X				X	

**Target Areas (See more in-depth definitions within the introduction)*

- *Sensory Processing*-**SP**
- *Emotional Regulation*-**ER**
- *Executive Functioning*-**EF**
- *Joint Attention*-**JA**
- *Receptive Language*-**RL**
- *Expressive Language*-**EL**
- *Pragmatic Language*-**PL**
- *Perspective Taking*-**PT**

		Page	**SP**	**ER**	**EF**	**JA**	**RL**	**EL**	**PL**	**PT**
IN THE COMMUNITY	IN THE CAR									
	Set the Child Up for Success– Priming	56		X	X		X		X	X
	Debriefing	56		X	X		X		X	X
	Same but Different	56		X	X				X	X
	Be a Kind Commuter	56			X					X
	What Can I Guess About Others?	57							X	X
	Social Lotto	57							X	X
	Share Your Feelings	57		X				X		X
	STOP and Breathe	57	X	X						
	AT THE MALL									
	Why Are We Here?	58		X	X			X	X	X
	Asking for Help	58		X				X	X	
	What's My Perspective?	58		X	X			X	X	X
	"Do You See What I See?"	59			X	X			X	X
	Coping with Emotions	59		X	X				X	X
	Hold the Door, Please	59		X		X			X	X
	AT THE PLAYGROUND OR PARK									
	Sharing is Caring	60				X		X	X	X
	Who Should I Play With?	60		X					X	X
	Sharing Your Imagination	60				X		X		X
	Partner and Group Activities	60	X	X		X	X		X	
	AT THE GROCERY STORE									
	Grocery List	61			X		X			
	What Aisle?	61			X		X			
	What's Cooking?	61			X					X
	EATING OUT									
	Step by Step	62		X	X		X			
	What Are You Going to Have?	62			X				X	X
	Social Secret Agent	62							X	X
	Master Chef for the Day	62			X			X		X
	AT THE DOCTOR'S OFFICE									
	Easing Fears	63		X					X	
	Do a Practice Run	63		X					X	
	Guessing Your Stats	63			X					
	AT THE MOVIES									
	Preshow	64			X					X
	Quiet in the Theater	64	X				X		X	X
	Movie Critic	64			X			X		X
	The Spotlight's on You	64						X	X	X

*Target Areas (See more in-depth definitions within the introduction)

- *Sensory Processing*-**SP**
- *Emotional Regulation*-**ER**
- *Executive Functioning*-**EF**
- *Joint Attention*-**JA**
- *Receptive Language*-**RL**
- *Expressive Language*-**EL**
- *Pragmatic Language*-**PL**
- *Perspective Taking*-**PT**

IN THE COMMUNITY

	Page	SP	ER	EF	JA	RL	EL	PL	PT
AROUND THE NEIGHBORHOOD									
Exploring Your World	65			X	X			X	
Who Are the People in the Neighborhood?	65			X				X	X
Neighborhood Niceties	65		X				X	X	X
Safety First: Don't Talk to Strangers	65		X					X	
SPORTS EVENTS									
Playing Ball	66		X	X				X	
Watching Sports	66		X					X	X
Building Emotional Vocabulary: A Sport in Itself!	66		X				X	X	X
GET OUT IN NATURE									
Nature Hunt	67		X					X	
Find Your Green Thumb	67		X	X					
Get Artsy	67			X					
Listening Walk	67	X	X						

HOLIDAYS AND SPECIAL EVENTS

HOLIDAYS AND SPECIAL EVENTS

	Page	SP	ER	EF	JA	RL	EL	PL	PT
GOVERNMENT AND NATIONAL HOLIDAYS									
It Takes a Village	70		X	X					X
Model Citizen	70			X					X
Crowds and Noisy Places	70	X	X					X	X
MOTHER'S DAY/FATHER'S DAY									
Showing Love to Mom/Dad	71		X	X					X
Queen or King for the Day	71		X	X					X
Happy Helpers	71		X	X		X			X
HALLOWEEN									
Costume Detective	72		X					X	X
Pumpkins Can Show Feelings!	72		X					X	
Ghouls and Goblins	72		X	X				X	X
Trick-or-Treat	72		X	X				X	
THANKSGIVING									
Giving Back	73		X						X
Planning a Meal	73		X	X			X		
Sensing Your Senses	73	X	X						
OTHER MAJOR HOLIDAYS									
Holiday Gift Giving	74		X	X					X
Charity Begins at Home	74		X						X
Bigger than a Breadbox	74			X					X
Teaching the Skills	74		X	X		X		X	

**Target Areas (See more in-depth definitions within the introduction)*

- *Sensory Processing*-**SP**
- *Emotional Regulation*-**ER**
- *Executive Functioning*-**EF**
- *Joint Attention*-**JA**
- *Receptive Language*-**RL**
- *Expressive Language*-**EL**
- *Pragmatic Language*-**PL**
- *Perspective Taking*-**PT**

HOLIDAYS AND SPECIAL EVENTS

	Page	SP	ER	EF	JA	RL	EL	PL	PT
BIRTHDAY PARTIES									
Shopping for Others	76					X		X	X
Goodie Bags	76		X	X			X		X
Thoughtful Words	76		X			X			X
Pretend Party	77		X	X		X		X	
Birthday Letter to Yourself	77		X	X					
Thinking About the Gift Giver	77						X	X	X
DINNER PARTIES									
Helping the Host	78		X	X		X			X
Act It Out	78		X	X		X			X
Party Tricks	78		X	X			X		
VACATION PLANNING AND ORGANIZATION									
Itinerary, Please!	79		X	X		X		X	
Tour Guide	79		X	X		X			
Sticking to a Schedule	79		X	X					
VACATION FUN									
How Are They Connected?	80							X	X
Special Memories	80		X				X		
Document and Tell Stories	80		X	X			X		
New Places, New People	81							X	X
"Say Cheese!"	81		X					X	X
"Name That Tune" and Other Car Games	81				X		X		X

BRIDGING HOME AND SCHOOL

BRIDGING HOME AND SCHOOL

	Page	SP	ER	EF	JA	RL	EL	PL	PT
SCHOOL DAYS-PLANNING AHEAD									
What Do You Need?	84		X	X		X		X	
Proactive Feel-Good Breaks	84	X	X	X					
Visualize the Day Ahead	84		X	X		X			
GETTING READY FOR SCHOOL									
Match the Picture	85		X	X		X			
Prepped and Ready	85		X	X		X			
Watching the Clock	85			X		X			
Special "Love Notes"	85		X		X				
HOMEWORK TIME									
Grand Central Station	86		X	X					
Places and Spaces	86	X	X	X					
Homework Schedule	86	X	X	X		X			
Backpack and Binder Prepper	86			X					

**Target Areas (See more in-depth definitions within the introduction)*

- *Sensory Processing*-**SP**
- *Emotional Regulation*-**ER**
- *Executive Functioning*-**EF**
- *Joint Attention*-**JA**
- *Receptive Language*-**RL**
- *Expressive Language*-**EL**
- *Pragmatic Language*-**PL**
- *Perspective Taking*-**PT**

BRIDGING HOME AND SCHOOL

	Page	**SP**	**ER**	**EF**	**JA**	**RL**	**EL**	**PL**	**PT**
A "WHOLE-CHILD" TEAM APPROACH									
Informational Letters	*87*	*X*	*X*	*X*	*X*	*X*	*X*	*X*	*X*
Orientation, Please	*87*		*X*	*X*	*X*			*X*	
Build Rapport	*87*		*X*						*X*
SUCCESSFUL SCHOOL DAYS									
Schedules and Routines	*88*		*X*	*X*				*X*	
Make it Visual	*88*		*X*	*X*				*X*	
Celebrate Strengths	*88*		*X*	*X*	*X*		*X*		
Processing Time	*88*		*X*	*X*		*X*			
Soothing Spaces	*89*	*X*	*X*						
Smooth Transitions	*89*		*X*	*X*					
Count Down	*89*	*X*	*X*	*X*				*X*	
PRE-GAME PRACTICE FOR RECESS									
Time to Regulate!	*90*	*X*	*X*						
The Power of Play	*90*			*X*	*X*	*X*		*X*	*X*
Be a Helicopter	*90*		*X*					*X*	*X*
Friendship Bench	*90*		*X*		*X*				*X*
SCHOOLWIDE KINDNESS									
Pay It Forward	*91*		*X*						*X*
It's Raining Kindness!	*91*		*X*				*X*		*X*
Learning Buddies	*91*		*X*						*X*
One-Minute Hellos	*91*		*X*				*X*	*X*	*X*
FIELD TRIPS, ASSEMBLES AND SPECIAL EVENTS									
Plan, Practice, Proceed, and Review	*92*		*X*	*X*		*X*		*X*	
Be Prepared…for Change!	*92*		*X*	*X*		*X*		*X*	
Making Connections to the Curriculum	*92*			*X*		*X*		*X*	
VOLUNTEERING AND GETTING INVOLVED									
Coffee Club	*94*		*X*		*X*	*X*	*X*	*X*	*X*
Sibling Support	*94*		*X*		*X*				*X*
Childcare Exchange	*94*		*X*	*X*		*X*		*X*	
Busy Parents Can Help Too!	*94*			*X*	*X*		*X*		
Volunteer Extraordinaire	*95*			*X*		*X*		*X*	*X*
Resourceful Resource Finder	*95*			*X*			*X*		
Play Date Host	*95*		*X*		*X*				
RECAPPING THE SCHOOL DAY									
Daily Communication	*96*		*X*					*X*	
Challenge of the Day	*96*		*X*	*X*			*X*		
Highlights of the School Day	*96*		*X*	*X*			*X*		

PART TWO
ACTIVITIES

AT HOME

START THE DAY

My Morning Schedule

To help develop more independence and executive functioning skills, such as planning and sequencing, help your child make a visual morning schedule of the steps involved with getting ready for the day. First, go over the steps involved, such as getting dressed, eating breakfast, brushing teeth, feeding the dog, etc. Then make visuals of these activities by drawing them, gathering pictures/icons from the internet, or taking actual photos of the child doing each activity. Place these on a board or something that is easily accessible. Make one column that says "to do" and one that says "done." Each morning, reference the schedule together. As each task is completed, the child can move the activity to the "done" column.

Intention of the Day

First thing in the morning, help your child pick an intention, or something to focus on for the day (e.g., "I will try a new game at recess today," "I will help around the house," "I will take a break when I get frustrated"). If needed, write or draw some of the intentions that have benefits and have the child make a choice from those options. Refer to the Sample Intentions on page 131.

Job Talk: *"You help be the planner."*

Backup Plan

Each morning, think of the day's activities, and discuss what is *expected* for each activity. Map situations that might be difficult, such as waiting in line at the grocery store or not being able to go to the park if it is raining. Make a backup plan for what to do if something changes. For example, if it rains, you can go to the movies instead of the park.

START THE DAY

HOME

Body Check-In

Wake up five to ten minutes earlier than usual and do a body scan together, helping your child focus on each part of their body and noticing how it feels. Breathe and relax each part of the body. Help them determine any sensations they might be feeling (e.g., cold, sweaty, tense muscles, belly growling) and try to label those sensations with an emotion word (e.g., hungry, calm, sleepy). Use the list of Sensation Words on page 132 and the Emotion Words on page 135.

Weather Detective

Have your child look outside to see what the weather is like and say what clues can be noticed. Clouds? Sun? Rain? Help your child decide what to wear based on those clues. For example, if it's cloudy and cold, do they need a sweater?

▶ **To Expand:** Have your child make a guess about the day ahead. Will they play outside for recess? Will they need an umbrella or a jacket? Will soccer practice be cancelled?

Job Talk: *"You be the weather reporter."*

Time to Wake Up

If your child struggles to get out of bed in the morning, practice using various regulation tools together to increase alertness. Some examples are stretching, exercising, taking a shower, face washing, or thinking about something to look forward to.

▶ **To Expand:** Put a photo of the activities that work best on the nightstand as a reminder of what to try in the mornings.

Hidden Rules: 1. It is okay to wake up groggy or grouchy, but being rude or mean to others makes them feel uncomfortable. 2. We all experience changes that we cannot control, but it's expected that we control our reactions when we get frustrated or disappointed or that we ask for help if we need to.

RULES FOR HAVING FUN

Review the Rules

Have your child help you discover what is expected for having fun. You can also make a visual reminder. Sample rules for having fun:

1. Keep your brain thinking about the other people playing. Watch to figure out whose turn it is and how they are playing.
2. Keep your body connected to the players by facing them, keeping your body near the group, and not wandering off.
3. Use a friendly voice, words, or actions (e.g., take turns and share).

Fair Play

Teach your child how to play Rock-Paper-Scissors as a tool to resolve conflicts, such as which game to play, what rules to play by, or who should go first. Players form one of three shapes with their hands to determine who is the winner. The "rock" beats "scissors," the "scissors" beats "paper," and the "paper" beats "rock." If players use the same shape, they are tied and have to do it again.

▶ **To Expand:** Try other ways to settle or decide on something, such as flip a coin or draw straws.

Contributed by Leah Kuypers

Adding to the Fun

When interacting with others and the goal is to have fun, use the suggestion, *"Add to the fun,"* as a friendly way to encourage positive behavior and attitude. Use the term, *"Take away from the fun,"* to represent the opposite–an unfriendly way of playing. These phrases can help kids understand how their behavior affects other people. We all like to have fun, so let's do things to *add to the fun!*

▶ **To Expand:** Map out the specifics about what *adding to the fun* or *taking away from the fun* looks like for various activities.

Hidden Rules: 1. When you play by the rules, you *add to the fun*. Someone who cheats *takes away from the fun*. 2. When you are bored or don't want to play a game anymore, it is thoughtful to ask your friends if they want to finish the game or if they are ready to play something else. You don't just walk away.

ENCOURAGE PLAY WITH PEERS AND SIBLINGS

Contributed by Pamela Wolfberg

Special Space

Create a special space for your child to play with other children.

1. Make the space familiar, safe, and inviting for all the children.
2. Include some of your child's favorite things to be enjoyed with others.
3. Organize the space with boxes of favorite toys, activities, and themes.
4. Label the play boxes with visual symbols, such as a picture of a tent for a camp theme.

Special Time with Peers

Set up special times for your child to play with other children.

Designate times to play with peers on a frequent and consistent basis. For example, set up a regular play date with some of your child's friends for an hour after school on Tuesdays and Thursdays. Make it part of the schedule to build anticipation and help ensure that meetups happen on a regular basis.

Create a visual schedule to help the child transition to this play routine. See sample on page 117.

Have Fun!

Guide your child in mutually enjoyable play experiences.

1. Support finding common ground, building on their unique fascinations and favorite materials. For example, if your child likes trains, they can ask the other children if they would like to play trains.
2. Follow the child's lead, allowing them to set the pace and flow of the experience. Start by connecting small trains and pushing them along a train track. You can add blocks to build tunnels and bridges, or you can add small boxes and toy figures to create a town.

Play Routines

Structure play sessions with consistent and pleasurable routines.

Opening routine: Start with a brief hello, guidelines for playing together, and an age-appropriate song or cheer. For example, have children place their hands one on top of the other, reach up, and yell, "Let's play!"

Guided play: Follow the opening routine and set aside a longer period (30–45 minutes) for play.

Closing routine: End with cleanup, a snack, and a goodbye song or cheer.

Hidden Rules: 1. Everyone loves to play with their favorite toy or focus on their area of interest. If you pay attention to someone else's interests, they will probably do the same for you. 2. Siblings have feelings too, and although it can be a struggle to get along at times, you need to think about their feelings so they will think about yours, too.

PRETEND PLAY

Dress-up

For young children, fill a box with dress-up clothes. Encourage your child to use imagination and pretend to be someone or something different. You can join in the fun and dress up, too. For example, if the child is the doctor, dress up and pretend to be the patient. If they pretend to be an animal, storybook character, or family member, help them understand their character's perspective to really play the part.

Pretend Play: Boxes, Boxes, and More Boxes

Kids love making houses, stores, lemonade stands, castles, go-carts, and rockets out of large cardboard boxes. Encourage pretend play to build imagination and *flexible thinking*. Have your child invite friends or siblings to join in the play, or pretend with their stuffed animals to help expand his perspective taking and conversation skills.

▶ **To Expand:** You can make a written script to help your child practice using phrases, such as: "Want to go for a ride?" "Would you like to have some lemonade?" "Should we go to the moon or the stars?"

***Job Talk:** "Are you the host?"*

Building a Fort

Put sheets over the top of a table to make it dark underneath. Put blankets on the floor with pillows and flashlights. Pretend to have a party, picnic, or sleepover with your child's favorite stuffed animals, or invite a sibling, neighbor, or caregiver in for a visit. Have your child practice being a host, greet others, and invite them in. If you pretend to go camping, set up camp and then prompt your child to pretend what might happen next (e.g., picnic or hike followed by s'mores).

Role-Play

Make cards listing different social situations (e.g., going to a birthday party or inviting a friend to join your game) and role-play them. You can use props, like puppets or stuffed animals, to role-play and problem solve. For example, help your child make a puppet show related to a social situation, having them use the puppets to act it out. Some kids find it easier to talk if they are using a stuffed animal or puppet.

▶ **To Expand:** Use stuffed animals that represent different emotions, and ask them to have the animal tell you about their day or emotional state.

Hidden Rules: 1. When someone comes to your house to play, it is friendly to let them choose the game to play. 2. If you play with a game, it's helpful to put it away after you are done so the pieces don't get lost. That way you can play with it again.

INDOOR ANTI-BOREDOM

No Voice Needed

Play games with your child without using your voice to increase awareness of nonverbal clues by assigning one person to be the guider and one to be the builder. For example, build a block tower and have the guide use nonverbal cues to show the others where to place the blocks, such as by using eye gaze, pointing fingers, or other body parts. Take turns being the guider and the builder, so your child gets practice in both using and following nonverbal cues. You can also play "Watch My Eyes," a game in which you hide a favorite toy, then help them find it by only using your eyes to give clues, then switching roles to give them practice with both points of view.

Job Talk: *"You be the guider/builder."*

Treasure Hunt

Practice following directions by placing clues around the house and have your child hunt for them to find the final prize or answer. For example, "The first clue is on top of the large appliance that keeps food cold." At the refrigerator, there is another clue that might state something like, "The next clue is under the large pillow that you like to snuggle with," or "You can find the next clue by the jar with the sweet round treats." If the child doesn't read, use photos to direct them to the next clue or read the clues out loud.

▶ **To Expand:** Use nonverbal feedback, such as smiling or nodding, to indicate if your child is headed to the right place.

Job Talk: *"Help me be a detective."*

Job Talk: *"You be the question-asker, and I'll be the question-answerer."*

Would You Rather?

Practice asking questions and showing interest and curiosity about others by playing the game, "Would You Rather?" Ask questions like, "Would you rather eat mushrooms or spinach?" "Would you rather go camping or skiing?" "Would you rather watch a baseball game or go to the movies?" See sample "Would You Rather?" questions on page 123.

▶ **To Expand:** Have your child answer why or why not, and have them ask you similar questions.

Hidden Rules: 1. Everyone gets bored sometimes, but it's important that you keep those bored feelings as private thoughts so you don't make other people feel bad. 2. You can learn a lot about someone else's thoughts by watching their face and body to determine what they might be thinking or feeling. 3. When playing games, be careful to monitor your personal space. Don't get too close to others unless you make sure it's okay with them. Watching their facial expressions and body language will help you determine how close you can get.

CHORES

Vacuuming

Play a game about which piece of furniture or object needs to be moved next in order for you to be able to vacuum the floor or carpet. Move the vacuum cleaner near pieces of furniture and use gestures (e.g., smiles, thumbs up, or thumbs down) to show which one needs to be moved. With the noise of the vacuum, it's crucial to understand gestures and facial expressions if you can't hear the words.

Job Talk: *"Can you be the furniture mover?"*

Whose Clothes?

Ask your child to sort the laundry with you and make a logical guess about which clothes belong to which family member. Help them use the information that is available (e.g., size, colors, and style) to determine which clothes belong to whom. Who likes to wear dresses? Whose favorite color is purple? This encourages thinking about others and builds problem-solving skills.

Job Talk: *"You be the house cleaner."*

Chore Detective

Tell your child that you are going to play a game similar to "I Spy." Have them be a detective and look for areas in the house that need cleaning or tidying up. Make a list of the things they can do without help, things you can do together, and things that need to be done by an adult. You can *add to the fun* by using a magnifying glass or funny hat so your child feels like a real detective.

▶ **To Expand:** Have your child picture what it should look like when it's done; for example, picture what the bed looks like when it is made. Have them start with the things they can do without help. As the tasks get more difficult, provide more support, such as adding a photo to show the job when it's done so that you always set your child up for success.

*See page 134 for a list of age-appropriate chores.

CHORES

Clear Vision for a Clean Future

Take photos of what you expect a room to look like when it's clean or the toy or book area when straightened. Post it for your child to see. When it is time to clean, ask them to "match the picture." This activity helps build situational awareness and the ability to visualize what a task should look like when completed.

Contributed by Sarah Ward

Job Talk: *"You be the bed-maker/ room-cleaner."*

Partner Chores

Help your child think of chores that are easier to get done with a partner to practice problem solving and teamwork. Then have them ask a family member to team up to get it done together. For example, ask someone to hold the dustpan so you can sweep up the piles, or ask if they will be the dish dryer if you are the dish washer.

Where Does It Belong?

Place a photo, drawing, or written word on the outside of drawers (clothing, kitchen, bathroom, etc.) to show where things belong. This allows your child to be more independent when putting things away and *follow the plan* for organization by putting their PJs in the PJ drawer or the clean bowls where the bowls go, etc.

Hidden Rules: 1. It is considered unsanitary to eat off a dirty plate. Make sure plates are clean before setting them on the table. 2. If you have to vacuum, first ask if it's okay to turn on the vacuum so you are not disturbing somebody who might be sleeping, watching TV, or reading. 3. Learning to do chores is just as important as learning schoolwork.

FURRY FRIENDS

Animals Help Cope with Emotions

Some people find that cuddling with a furry friend creates a positive mood. When your child is feeling sad or upset, suggest curling up with their pet and take a break. Your child can talk to the pet and share their feelings. Pets are great listeners and the most nonjudgmental members of the family.

Pets: Help Them, Help Us!

If you have pets, have your child help care for them to build responsibility and perspective taking. Create a food and water schedule to follow. Make a list of additional activities that the pet needs that they can provide, such as walking, petting, and bathing.

▶ **To Expand:** Help them be aware of the nonverbal clues that show how the pet might be feeling. For example, when the cat is hungry, it might stand near its bowl, or a dog might wag its tail when happy and ready to play.

Job Talk: *"You be the groomer/dog walker/ brusher/feeder."*

Job Talk: *"You be the dog trainer."*

New Tricks

Kids love to teach dogs tricks like sit, shake, and roll over. Help your child train their dog or animal to do one of these tricks. Encourage them to guess what the dog is thinking to build perspective taking and awareness of nonverbal clues.

▶ **To Expand:** Refer to the Mood Meter on page 112 either during or after this activity and ask your child how they're feeling. Ask your child to identify how the dog might be feeling.

Emotional Benefits

Pets can help build emotional awareness and empathy, as well as being great companions and friends. Have your child watch the pet and try to read its nonverbal cues to determine how it feels or what it wants (e.g., Is it hungry or tired?). If a dog looks sad because you are leaving the house, talk about what might make it feel better (e.g., give it a toy to play with while you are gone).

Hidden Rules: 1. Sometimes pets don't like people to bother them when they are eating. 2. Always ask before petting someone else's dog or picking up their pet. 3. Pets need care and attention.

PHONE ETIQUETTE

HOME

Receiving a Call

Practice talking on the telephone with your child. Make sure they listen for important information–who is calling, who the person is calling for, etc. If your child does not understand what is being said, help them ask for clarification (e.g., "I can't hear you. Can you say that again?"). Start by using play phones to role-play, then practice on a real call with a familiar person.

Job Talk: *"Be a receptionist."*

Hand Signals

Create hand signals to help your child predict the expected wait time when on the phone. For example, create a visual chart with an open palm indicating, "I can talk about this later," a hand with the index finger pointing upward indicating, "I can talk about this in a minute," and a hand shaped like a cup indicating, "I can talk now. I just finished my call."

Contributed by Emily Rubin

Don't Be an Interruptosaurus!

Help your child notice when someone in your family is talking on the phone. What is the expected behavior? It is not a time to talk or ask for help, except in an emergency. This is similar to interrupting people in a conversation. You can use the vocabulary "Your words are bumping into my words" or "Don't be an *interruptosaurus*" to help them visualize how distracting interruptions can be. Practicing these skills ahead of time can decrease frustration when an important call comes in.

Talking on the Phone

Establish guidelines for use of the telephone and discuss them with the family. Are you going to bring phones to the dinner table? Can you text during family time? By creating and following your own family guidelines, you can prompt your child to think about the impact phone use has on other people and how it can make them feel. For example, explain that, if you are on your phone, it can show that you are not thinking about the people around you, and it might make them feel less important.

Contributed by Kari Dunn Buron

Hidden Rules: 1. When you answer the phone, say "Hello," and before you hang up, say "Goodbye." 2. Be careful about what time it is when you call people. Don't call early in the morning, during dinnertime, or late at night. 3. Never make prank phone calls; it is illegal, and you can get into serious trouble. 4. Keep your phone conversation short, and if the other person says they have to go, say goodbye and call back another time.

SHOWTIME

Be a Family Detective

Present your child with a choice of three familiar TV shows, and ask which show they think each member of the family would want to watch and why. This is a great activity for learning to think about others and what they like.

▶ **To Expand:** Help your child do a survey asking friends and families about their favorite TV shows and movies. The child can then compare their answers to their own family's favorites.

Who Gets to Pick?

Create a family tradition of watching a TV show or movie together. Make a schedule of who gets to pick the show each time. Have your child make a logical guess as to what show they think family members will pick when it is their turn. This provides practice in thinking about others and being flexible.

Job Talk: *"You be the detective!"*

Learning the Characters

During TV time, let your child choose a show. Suggest they identify one character in the show and explain who the character is and what that character's role is in the show. Help identify what this character likes or does not like and what their relationship is with the other characters on the show. This builds perspective taking and thinking about others and how they are related.

I See What You're Thinking

While watching a TV show or movie, make up games to help your child learn about their own or others' perspectives and perceptions. Talk out loud about thoughts and feelings that come up. Start by suggesting they think about the thoughts and feelings the characters/actors might be having, then identify their own thoughts and feelings about what they are watching. Finally, suggest they "turn the tables" and determine how you or others watching the show might be feeling. Do you share the same thoughts and feelings, or are they different?

Contributed by Michelle Garcia Winner

Hidden Rules: 1. When watching TV with other people, you won't always get to watch your favorite show. This is a time for being together and using your *flexible brain*. 2. Speak in a low voice while people are watching TV so they can hear the show. 3. It is always a good idea to ask before changing the channel. Grabbing the remote or changing the channel while someone is watching TV can make the person feel upset.

FAMILY TOGETHER TIME

HOME

A Picture Is Worth a Thousand Words

Pull out the family photo album and talk about activities and events in the pictures. Have your child practice looking at the nonverbal clues and identify the people in the photos and their relationships. Help them figure out the context (situation) of a photo, identify the body language, observe the facial expressions, and make a guess about how the people felt. For example, if it was a birthday party, whose party was it? Does it look like everyone is having fun?

▶ **To Expand:** Refer to the Mood Meter on page 112 either during or after this activity, and check in about how your child is feeling. If you don't have the Mood Meter nearby, ask them to describe how the activity makes them feel. For example, does seeing other people being happy make your child feel happy? Does seeing pictures of relatives who live far away make them feel sad?

Job Talk: *"Do you want to be an interviewer or a reporter?"*

Family Tree

You and your child can make a family tree or chart, using photos. Find a photo of each family member, and tape or glue it onto a piece of cardboard. Under the photo, write the name of the person and what that person likes. Have your child conduct interviews with family members to gain information. If appropriate, write a script of what to ask (e.g., "What's your favorite color?"). This is a great way to practice perspective taking—thinking about the thoughts and feelings of others.

Thinking About the Family

Make a list of things that family members like to do, then talk about things you can do together. Help your child draw a picture of themself and a family member doing an activity they both enjoy. Model telling stories about family members and things you did with them. Help them tell similar stories about family members and events. Sharing personal stories builds relationships and helps you gain a deeper understanding of who you are and where you come from.

Job Talk: *"You be the thinker."*

I Think I'm Thinking!

Our goal with young children is to help them become aware that they are having thoughts about things. Make it fun! When you and your child are together, do something very unexpected or silly. For instance, sit down on the floor while you're mixing cookie batter or stand on the couch when it's time to watch a movie together. Ask: "You're having a thought about me! What are you thinking?" Then reverse the idea. When your child is doing something wonderful, give a big smile and a hug and say, "I'm having a thought about you right now. I'm thinking you're so talented/terrific/generous, etc." Conversely, when your child is doing something unexpected, share your thoughts about the behavior: "I'm having a thought about you right now. I'm thinking you're supposed to be in bed and you're not. This makes me have uncomfortable thoughts about you."

Contributed by Michelle Garcia Winner

Hidden Rules: 1. Some people enjoy talking about their family and childhood. Others find that hard to do. If you ask somebody a question about their family and they change the subject, move on to another topic. 2. People's favorite activities often change with age. What someone liked to do last year might be different this year, so ask to make sure.

TALENT WANTED

Comic Relief

Jokes are a good way to teach the double meanings of words, "play on words," or puns, such as "I went to a seafood disco last week . . . and pulled a mussel." Practicing jokes at the dinner table or during a family talent show can help prepare your child for telling jokes to friends. See page 118 for a list of kid-friendly jokes. Humor can be used to build social connections and provide a tool for self-regulation. It can also be used as an icebreaker to initiate conversation.

Best in Show

Have your child teach your pet a trick. This will take lots of practice. Help them think about how to get the pet to cooperate and have a good time too. Your child and the pet can then perform the trick during a talent show or when people come over. Pets and animals can be used as an icebreaker or point of interest to facilitate social interactions for many children.

Job Talk: *"You be the dog trainer/groomer."*

Job Talk: *"You are the actor, and we are the audience."*

Family Skits

Make and act out a skit together as a family. Who is going to be which character? What is needed for the costumes? Who will be in the audience? Acting in a play or doing a skit is a great way to practice stepping into another person's shoes and thinking about what others might think about and how they act. Acting also involves using and understanding nonverbal language. For example, if you have to perform in a play and pretend to be an animal, you need to think about what that animal looks and acts like, then use those movements and gestures to act it (e.g., an elephant has a trunk and walks slowly on all four legs).

Job Talk: *"You be a musician/singer/performer."*

Start a Band

Hang a sheet or blanket in a doorway, grab a toy microphone or a hairbrush, and pretend to put on a concert. Working with multiple people is harder than working with just one. Every person must pick an instrument (either real or imaginary), help select a song, then practice singing at the same time. Pay attention to how fast or slow you are singing, or how loud or soft everyone is. This type of activity helps to practice working together as a group and thinking about others.

Hidden Rules: 1. Telling the same joke over and over to the same people makes the joke less funny. 2. Don't tell jokes that make fun of other people or might be considered rude. 3. Being on stage is fun, but you need to share time and space, so that others don't think you are hogging airtime and not sharing the stage. 4. Pets are good for showing off talent, but make sure to treat them with respect and care.

Play is a fundamental right and vital to children's learning, development and inclusion in the culture of childhood. By providing genuine opportunities for play, we can help children access the joy and benefits these experiences afford.

—Pamela Wolfberg

ARTS AND CRAFTS

Drawing Conclusions

Draw pictures of faces with different mouths, eyebrows, eyes, and noses. Talk about the difference in the faces and the feelings/emotions that they show. Discuss how a smile versus a frown or raised eyebrows versus wrinkled eyebrows, can change what message or expression the face shows. Model the expression yourself and encourage your child to do the same. This is great for learning to express and identify emotions.

Handmade Thoughts

Help your child make friendship cards or draw a picture for a family member or a friend. Have them think about the colors the person likes, and write something nice that is specific to their relationship with the person. Do they have a pet to draw or ask about? Has the person been somewhere fun that your child could ask about?

▶ **To Expand:** Refer to the Mood Meter on page 112 either during or after this activity, and check in how your child is feeling. If you don't have the Mood Meter nearby, ask them to describe how the activity made them feel.

Job Talk: *"Be a Social Thinker."*

Inside Others' Minds

Trace the body of a friend or family member on a sheet of butcher paper. In the space where the head or brain is, have your child draw things they know the person likes to think about. If they don't know what to draw, suggest interviewing the person or asking questions to find out. If drawing is difficult, suggest cutting photos from a magazine that the person might like. This will help your child learn to think about the thoughts and desires of others.

ARTS AND CRAFTS

Drawing a Snapshot of a Child's Point of View

Have your child draw or use other forms of art to show and explain various social situations in his life. Encourage them to use thinking and talking bubbles to show what the people might be thinking or saying. A drawing can help them express feelings, show what happened in a situation, or reveal his point of view.

Job Talk: *"Do you want to be the drawer or the writer?"*

Pretend Pen Pals

Set up boxes around the house and help your child write letters to family members and put them in the "mailboxes." If they need help, create a template, show an example, or have them draw pictures. Help them think about things to share from their own life, including thoughtful comments and questions. Suggest they tell you when there is mail so you or a sibling can get the letters and write back.

▶ **To Expand:** Refer to the Mood Meter on page 112 to have your child share their feelings when receiving mail.

Job Talk: *"You're the writer."*

Visualizing With the End in Mind

Set out a yellow ("Slow down and get ready"), green ("Do"), and red ("Done") piece of construction paper. Print a picture of a craft you are going to do. Tell your child that you start a task by thinking about what it will look like when you are done. Place the picture on the red paper and look at it to decide what you need to do to make the end product look like that. Write the steps or draw pictures of what you need to do on the green paper. Then look at the end picture and decide which materials you will need to gather to make the craft. Write the list of materials on the yellow paper. Don't just give the child the materials, have them imagine the materials, think about where to find them, and then collect the supplies. See page 116 for a sample worksheet of "Get Ready, Do, and Done."

Contributed by Sarah Ward and Kristen Jacobsen

Hidden Rules: 1. Don't draw on someone else's artwork unless you have permission. 2. Put crayons and markers back in the container when you are done using them so they don't make a mess or dry out and so that others can find them.

IN THE KITCHEN

Service with a Smile

During TV or family time, have your child ask the people in the room if they would like anything to eat. See if they can remember what the person ordered and bring it to them like a waiter. This is great for improving memory and thinking of others.

Job Talk: *"You be the waiter."*

Our Eyes Show Our Thoughts

Our eyes are powerful tools to help us understand the situation we are in. Following eye gaze can provide clues about what someone is thinking based on what that person is looking at. The following strategy, called "*thinking with your eyes*," is designed to suggest that we don't just *look* at things, we also *think* about what we're seeing. In various settings, practice this skill by making up games that don't include words. Keep it simple at first by having your child just follow your eye gaze, and then add complexity as you go along.

1. For example, when it's dinnertime, play, "What am I looking at?" while you're making dinner. Ask your child to follow your eye gaze to look toward where you're looking, then try to figure out what you might be looking at. Make it obvious at first (look at the refrigerator or the frying pan in your hand), and then refine things as you go along (look at an egg or the spatula on the counter).
2. Take this idea to the next level, and play, "What am I thinking about?" Again, look at different things, but this time ask your child to guess what you're thinking about. For instance, if you're looking at the pitcher of iced tea, you might be thinking about the fact that you're thirsty. If you're looking at the clock, you might be thinking about the time dinner will be ready.

Contributed by Michelle Garcia Winner

Surprise Snack

Help your child make a snack for the rest of the family. First, brainstorm what others might like (e.g., popcorn if they are watching a movie, a popsicle if it is hot outside, or soup if somebody is sick). Have your child serve the snacks and watch family members show appreciation with both their facial expressions and words. This builds positive reinforcement for thinking about others and taking their perspective.

Hidden Rules: 1. Close the refrigerator door after opening it. Leaving it open wastes energy and can make the food go bad. 2. Pour your milk, juice, and other drinks into a cup instead of drinking from the carton. 3. Wipe off the table or counter if you leave crumbs or a mess behind. 4. When the words "zapping" or "nuking" are used in the kitchen, it refers to cooking something in the microwave.

DINNER OR MEAL PREPARATION

Making Dinner Together

Have your child help prepare dinner once a week. Make index cards with photos (cut from magazines, coupons, or downloaded from the internet) to show the steps needed to make the meal (e.g., rolling out the pizza dough, spreading the sauce, sprinkling the cheese, baking the pizza, and then slicing it). You can even find picture recipes online. Using picture recipes builds sequencing skills that are an important component of executive functioning.

Job Talk: *"You can be the baker/cook/chef."*

Food for Thought: What's for Dinner?

Encourage your child to look around and make a guess about what is for dinner. What do they see? Smell? How is the table set? Suggest asking questions to get clues.

▶ **To Expand:** Once your child has guessed what you are having for dinner, have them help determine what will be needed to go with the meal. If you are having bread, should we get the butter out? If it's hamburgers, do we need ketchup? If soup, are spoons needed? This will help your child develop observation and *social detective* skills, as well as inferencing.

Job Talk: *"Can you be the table setter?"*

Get Ready, Do, Done!

Start with a picture of what a food item looks like when prepared and ready to eat (e.g., What does a ham sandwich look like when it's done?). 1. Figure out what is needed to make it, and get all the ingredients (GET READY). 2. What will we need to do with the ingredients to put the sandwich together? (DO). 3. When you are finished, look at it to make sure it matches the picture or what you hoped it would look like. Eat it! (DONE). See page 116 for a sample worksheet of "Get Ready, Do, and Done." Providing a visual system like this provides a mental image that is needed for executive functioning skills.

Contributed by Sarah Ward and Kristen Jacobsen

Formal Dinners

Occasionally, have a formal dinner with just your family, using cloth napkins, name cards, and formal place settings. You can have formal dinners once a month or more, if you wish, and if you have the time. The big payoff is that when you have company for dinner or are invited out, your child will be familiar with the concept of "formal" dinner and be better able to handle differences like seating arrangements and cloth napkins.

Contributed by Kari Dunn Buron

Hidden Rules: 1. Wash your hands to make sure they are clean before helping to prepare food. 2. It's a good idea to keep your hands and mouth out of the food when you are preparing it for others. 3. While cooking or handling food, pull your hair back or wear a hat. If hair gets in the food, it is unsanitary, and it will also make other people feel uncomfortable.

AT THE TABLE

Talking Stick

Bring a microphone, spoon, or spatula to the table. Take turns passing it around, letting each family member use it as a microphone to "check in" about how their day went. Model giving one or two positives about the day and also something that was difficult or disappointing. For example, "I was happy when I finished a big project at work today, but it took extra time, and I was frustrated that it delayed me in getting home on time." Use the Mood Meter on page 112 to help your child identify how they felt throughout the day.

Job Talk: *"I will be the talker, and you can be the listener."*

Dinner Schedule

Make a visual schedule showing the expectations for dinner or mealtime. The visuals can be photos, drawings, or written words for each step involved in what you would like your child to do during mealtime (e.g., setting table, eating food, clearing plates, etc.). See the dinnertime schedule on page 115 for an example.

Job Talk: *"Be a listener."*

Listening With the Whole Body

Mealtime is a great opportunity to practice listening with the whole body. This is a good way to break down an abstract concept and provide an opportunity to practice in a small, structured setting. Have your child use their eyes to look at the person speaking; use their ears to hear the words; keep their hands, feet, and body still; keep their mouth quiet; use their brain to think about what the person is saying; and use their heart to care about what they are hearing and about the person who is talking. If these skills are difficult and hinder actual listening, have your child develop ways to make them easier (e.g., do chair push-ups while listening), and discuss ways your child can advocate to tell others that moving actually helps them listen better or that looking directly in someone's eyes is a distractor. See Whole Body Listening visual on page 122.

Conversation Cards

Make and cut out conversation cards and place them in the middle of the table. Write open-ended questions, such as, "What was the most fun part of your day?" or "What did you do in your after-school class today?" During dinner, take turns picking up a card and asking and answering the questions. Practicing conversations at home (with visual prompts) helps with everyday conversation at school and beyond. Open-ended questions, rather than yes/no questions, allow expansion on topics.

See sample conversation cards on page 113.

AT THE TABLE

HOME

Table Guidelines

Set expectations for what behaviors to use at the dinner table, both at home and in public (e.g., chewing with your mouth closed or waiting until others are done eating before asking to be excused). Some rules are universal to all settings, such as chewing with your mouth closed, while others pertain more to eating in public places (e.g., such as staying seated during the meal), depending on how strict the rules are at your home. Either way, your child should be aware of what might be expected or unexpected when eating with others. Have your child watch and learn from others.

▶ **To Expand:** Make a game out of it by having the child observe others and notice when other people at the table are following or not following family table manners.

"Eye See You"

We can determine what someone is thinking about just by observing and determining what they are looking at (refer back to Michelle Garcia Winner's activity, "Our Eyes Show Our Thoughts"). Practice this skill by making up games that don't include words. For example,

1. When it's time to sit and eat, have one person be the "seat assigner," and have them use their eye gaze to show where everyone is supposed to sit.
2. When someone wants something passed to them at the table, have your child make their needs and wants known by using only gestures and eye contact.
3. Offer choices of food or drink (e.g., water or milk) and have the person indicate what they would like by looking at the desired item, no words allowed.

Wonder Questions

Make a written, visual cue or prompt for the type of questions that might be asked during dinnertime. Wh-questions (who, what, which, when, etc.) are great for wondering about others.

▶ **To Expand:** When your child is able to ask questions using the visual prompt, take it away and only present it if they struggle to remember how to start a sentence. See the Wonder Questions on page 114 for examples.

Hidden Rules: 1. Don't "yuck" another person's "yum." Sometimes what you dislike is delicious to others. Don't make negative comments about someone else's food. 2. Ask before taking or eating from someone else's plate. 3. It is considered rude to reach over the table to get something. Instead, ask, "Pass it, please." 4. Be sure to keep your mouth closed while you are chewing food. Wait until you have swallowed your food to talk. 5. Wash your hands before eating a meal.

NIGHTTIME ROUTINE

How Was Your Day?

Start the bedtime routine early so you have time to talk with your child about how their day went. Ask them to share something that went well or something that might be on their mind that they may want to talk about. You will be amazed at how much more children share at this time of day. Most children will do anything to stay up, even share the activities of their day.

▶ **To Expand:** Use the list of emotion words on page 135 if your child needs help building emotional awareness and vocabulary.

Sweet Dreams

Before your child falls asleep, encourage them to think about things that make them happy and people they might want to dream about. Suggest trying to remember dreams so they can share them in the morning. Your child can practice telling stories about the fun they had while dreaming. Focusing on the positive before going to bed can calm the mind. Sharing our dreams is a fun topic for conversation.

Gratitude

Before bed, have your child recall one friend, family member, or person that they saw that day for whom they are thankful and then explain why. Provide a model or indirect verbal prompt by saying something like, "It was great to watch you play with your cousin today. I saw him share his toy with you. That must have made you feel thankful and happy." Help them see how relationships and people can add to their life. Modify the "I Am Thankful For" visual on page 120 if you want a visual support for this activity.

Nighttime Check-in

When asking your child about their day, use a rating scale so they can label the emotions they feel about the various things that happened. Providing a rating scale helps to break down abstract social and emotional behavior into something visual, concrete, and easy to talk about. You can use the following examples or you can make up your own scale, using your own words:

5 = This made me feel awesome!

4 = This made me feel very happy!

3 = This made me feel comfortable/okay.

2 = This made me irritated.

1 = This made me feel angry or mad.

See sample 5-point scale for nighttime routine on page 119.

Contributed by Kari Dunn Buron

NIGHTTIME ROUTINE

Body Scan

Use the Body Scan visual on page 133 to visually guide your child through a body scan. Start at the top of the body and have them "check the brain" to identify how their brain feels in that moment. Refer to the Body Scan visual for words that can be used to describe the sensations noticed. Continue the body scan by moving down their body, pausing at each body part, and encouraging them to notice and describe the way each body part feels. You can also use the Sensation Words on page 132.

Contributed by Kelly Mahler

Boxing Up Your Worries

If your child has worries, fears, or even just a lot of thoughts that keep them up at night, suggest writing them down on a piece of paper and putting them under their pillow or in a "worry box" to symbolize letting them go.

▶ **To Expand:** Purchase or make a "worry doll." Have your child tell the doll about their worries so the doll can take the worries for them. Then they can put the doll under their pillow and out of sight to sleep peacefully. This is a Guatemalan bedtime tradition.

Belly Breathing

When lying down for bed, help your child practice belly breathing as a tool for self-regulation. Put a book on their stomach and suggest watching it move up and down with each belly breath that goes in and out. For added fun, have them put a favorite stuffed animal on the belly to watch that go up and down instead of the book.

▶ **To Expand:** There are other ways to practice belly breathing, such as tracing a shape while breathing in and out (See Six Sides of Breathing on page 126), having the child put a hand on the belly, and using words to help your child think about their breathing, "I am breathing in; I am breathing out."

Hidden Rules: 1. Sleep is very important for your brain and body. 2. Electronics stimulate your brain and make it hard to fall asleep. Shut down screens at least thirty minutes before bedtime. 3. Bedtime is a time for winding down and being quiet. Closing your eyes and turning off the lights will help you fall asleep.

IN THE BATHROOM

Scrubbing is Loving

Help your child understand that good hygiene is important, not only for keeping clean and preventing the spread of germs, but also for conveying a message or impression to other people that we value ourselves. Teach them to wash their face, body, and hair, and to brush their teeth. Teach the importance of this during the early years so when your child becomes a teenager, this will already be a routine.

Job Talk: *"Be a good tooth brusher/face washer/etc."*

Make a Splash

If your child enjoys taking a bath, use this time as a teachable moment to practice sharing imaginary thoughts. Many activities can be used for imaginary play during bathtime, such as making the bubbles into a mountain of snow or turning the washcloth into a boat that sinks in the water. You can also use toys, sing songs, or play hide-and-seek with the washcloth to engage and have fun while getting clean.

Mindful Toothbrushing

Mindfulness activities are good for training the brain and body to pause and be aware of the present moment. You can practice during simple activities such as brushing your teeth. Help your child practice this by having them slowly breathe in and out while brushing teeth. Count to 50 as they brush. Have your child relax their neck and jaw and feel the bristles on the teeth, gums, and tongue, noticing how it feels.

Job Talk: *"Can you be a bather/scrubber?"*

Following the Steps

If your child has difficulty following all the sequences of bathing, brushing teeth, washing hands, etc., make a visual checklist or chart to aid with proper hygiene. See the visual for brushing teeth on page 121. This will help your child complete these tasks in a timely manner and be more independent.

Hidden Rules: 1. Close the door when you are using the bathroom. 2. Always knock and wait to see if someone answers before opening a closed bathroom door. 3. Flush the toilet and wash your hands after using the bathroom, and don't talk about what you did in the bathroom. 4. Pull up your pants and zipper, and get your clothes straight before you leave the bathroom. 5. Avoid discussing your bathroom activities or asking others about theirs; it is considered private.

It's important to become mindfully aware of how our body is feeling in the present moment so that we can bridge and build social and emotional skills throughout the day.

—Kelly Mahler

READING AND STORY TIME

Stepping into the Character's Shoes

Begin by choosing simple books with one main character. After reading a book with your child, talk about the character(s). Make guesses about what the characters do or don't like, about how they feel, and about what the characters in the book think about each other.

▶ **To Expand:** Pull out some oversized shoes and label them with a character's name. Have your child step into those shoes and describe what that character might be feeling or thinking, or what they might want to do. For example, if they are reading a Harry Potter book, suggest thinking about what Harry likes to think and talk about (e.g., quidditch and owls). Understanding the perspective of the character in a book is essential for reading comprehension and also helps with real-life social competence.

Wordless Picture Books

Find picture books without writing (wordless books). Have your child look at the pictures and try to figure out what's going on. What are the clues? Have them tell you the story. Occasionally, pick a picture from the book and ask what they think will happen to the character immediately, within the next ten minutes, after an hour, and tomorrow. This is great for increasing expressive language and critical thinking.

Contributed by Sarah Ward.

Job Talk: *"You be the predictor."*

Job Talk: *"You be the guesser."*

Guessing What the Book is About

Take out a book that your child is not familiar with and have them look at the cover image and guess what the book is about. While reading the book, have them guess what's going to happen next. Looking for clues and making inferences about what will happen helps children in school and social situations.

Reading and Literacy

Find books about children or characters who have social problems or differences that make their lives difficult in some way. Talking about fictional characters with social problems is far less personal than talking about our own problems. You and your child can come up with creative and fun ideas for how the fictional character can solve the problem. This practice can make it easier for a child to eventually solve some problems of their own.

Contributed by Kari Dunn Buron

READING AND STORY TIME

HOME

Tone of Voice

When reading aloud to your child, use a different tone of voice for each character. Discuss how that character might be feeling based on the tone you use. Change the tone from time to time for the same character and situation. Help them identify the difference in how that character might be feeling when the tone is changed. Recognizing tone of voice is a part of being able to understand nonverbal language.

▶ **To Expand:** For children who struggle with reading, try using audio books. Listen to the way narrators use different tones of voice for different characters. Encourage your child to use different tones when reading aloud to you, based on how they think the character might be feeling.

What Would You Do?

When reading to your child, pause from time to time and ask what they think might happen next. How would they handle the situation? After reading along and determining what actually happened in the book, compare it to what they said. If it was different, ask which version they like better. This can be especially helpful when reading fiction books and working on building imagination and perspective taking.

Job Talk: *"You be the storyteller."*

The Best Listeners

If your child struggles with reading and becomes nervous or anxious, have them read to your dog or pet. This provides good practice with nonjudgmental listeners, and can build your child's confidence in reading.

▶ **To Expand:** Many animal shelters have reading programs that allow children to read to shelter animals. Look for one in your area, or start one yourself.

Contributed by Ruth Prystash

Book Club

Start a book club with your family or friends. Make a list of books that are age appropriate for your child and choose a book that is related to the skills you are trying to teach them. Develop some questions for them to think about before reading the book (e.g., "What are the main relationships in the book?" or "Who had a difficult situation and how did they handle it?"). After reading the book, get together with the others who read the book to discuss the questions they have been thinking about.

Hidden Rules: 1. When someone is reading to you, try to pay attention and focus on the story. 2. Be careful with books so you don't rip them when you turn the page. 3. Sometimes, characters in a book will use terms that you don't understand, like "It's raining cats and dogs." It's okay to ask what those things mean. 4. It's okay to read aloud to yourself as long as you don't disturb others near you.

SEND THOUGHTFUL LETTERS

Stay in Touch

Have your child develop a relationship with another child who doesn't live near you by sending letters or emails to each other. This could be a cousin, a friend who moved away, or a pen pal. Have them tell stories about what is going on in their life, ask questions about the other person, and think of topics that the recipient would want to know about. If your child struggles with writing, you can scribe for them and let them draw pictures.

Letter of Apology

When your child has a challenging encounter with another child or sibling, or does something unexpected with an adult at school or elsewhere, have them discuss what happened. Then help them write a letter to apologize for any actions they regret or that made the other person feel uncomfortable. A common formula for an apology includes:

1. Stating what they are sorry for: "I am sorry for ______."
2. Stating what they will do next time: "Next time, I will ______."
3. Asking for forgiveness: "Will you forgive me?"

▶ **To Expand:** Add another step that includes the child thinking about how the other person felt before and after the apology.

Job Talk: *"Can you be the apologizer?"*

Global Thinker

If your child is asking about something on the news that is going on in another part of the country or world, such as a natural disaster, or if there is something devastating that has happened to someone, help them write a letter to express their feelings and concern for what the person must be going through. Maybe there is a person or organization to whom they can send the letter. If they have trouble writing, maybe they can send a hand-drawn card to show that they are thinking about the person and the situation they are in.

Get-Well Wishes

When you send a note or take food to someone who is sick, tell your child what you are doing. Explain that it's important to help others. Letting people know that you are thinking about them is a kind thing to do and builds empathy.

▶ **To Expand:** Encourage your child to write a letter, sign the card you bought, or help drop off the food.

Hidden Rules: 1. Writing letters shows thoughtfulness to others and makes them feel appreciated. 2. Most people do not care about your handwriting, but if writing is difficult, type it out or ask someone to write for you. 3. Drawings can be just as special as a handwritten letter.

FAMILY CONNECTIONS

Family Meetings

Take time to gather the family together on a weekly basis to share news, go over the calendar for the upcoming week, and talk about any challenges that might need family members to problem-solve as a team. Remember to acknowledge any accomplishments and show appreciation or gratitude for each other. Family meetings can be a good way to stay connected, share information, and solve problems, just like any other groups that work together on a regular basis.

▶ **To Expand:** Take turns running the meeting if your child is old enough to do so. Have one person be in charge of bringing snacks to the meeting. Add in some family fun after the meeting.

Box of Kindness

Make a box that is labeled "Acts of Kindness" or "Nice Things People Do." Put index cards or small pieces of paper nearby so that it's easy for family members to write big or little things that each person has done to be kind or helpful to each other. These can be as simple as noticing when someone makes a snack for the other person or when one person lets another have control of the remote control while watching TV. Put the notes in the box. Review all the notes at your family meeting or at dinnertime.

▶ **To Expand:** Another option is to put a penny or marble in the jar for every kind act and try to fill it. If you put money in the jar, consider donating the funds to a charitable organization.

Job Talk: *"You be the noticer."*

Job Talk: *"Can you be the turn-taker?"*

Play Together to Stay Together

Take the time to play games together, either as a family or alone with your child. Simple games such as Uno or Go Fish can be played while waiting for dinner, after a family meeting, when needing a break from homework or chores, or right after school as a time to connect and unwind. Games are an excellent way to practice turn-taking, regulation, perspective taking, and much more.

Hidden Rules: 1. If you are feeling lonely, it's okay to ask for some time with your parent or caregiver. Most of the time, it will help them feel better, too. 2. If you are not in the mood for family time, ask if you can have a break and join in later. 3. Families come in all shapes and sizes. If your parents are not around, look for another caring adult to spend time with (e.g., nanny, neighbor, older sibling, friend's parent, etc.).

CALM CASA

Spa Day

Set up a calm space with tranquil music, dim lighting, and maybe even aromatherapy for you and your child to have a "spa day" together. Offer hand and foot massages, back rubs, or even pedicures to bring on the relaxation from head to toe, just like at a real spa.

Job Talk: *"Can you be the relaxer?"*

Family Yoga

Model and introduce some basic yoga poses to your child to practice focus and balance, and incorporate stretching exercises into family fun. Some basic, common poses to try are Tree Pose, Downward Dog, Cat/Cow, Happy Baby, and Corpse Pose for deep relaxation. Yoga increases body awareness, integrates the body and mind, and provides relaxation and focus/mindfulness.

Calming Corner

Designate a place in the house for quiet time, calming down, or just plain chilling out. Have your child help pick where that place will be, and make sure it's big enough for multiple people. Have them help with the design and props (e.g., bean bag, lava lamp, photos of things that bring them joy and good feelings, scents, and music that make them feel calm, etc.). Note: This is not a place for "time out" or punishment. It's a place to gather and relax and calm down if needed.

▶ **To Expand:** Consider joining your child in their spot on a regular basis. Provide some extra relaxation by providing a hand or foot massage or by doing something that they love to do, such as reading together.

Job Talk: *"Are you ready to be a sleeper/eater/exerciser?"*

Basic Needs for Success

Talk with your child on a daily basis about how their body and brain feel when taking care of themself and making healthy choices. Discuss how sleep, food, water, and exercise help the brain and body function and feel good. Talk about the choices that you make on a daily basis, about how you sometimes forget to make these healthy choices, and about how that feels (e.g., "I stayed up too late last night, and I'm having a hard time thinking today. I will go to bed early tonight.").

▶ **To Expand:** Make sure to discuss other healthy choices, such as connecting with other people, getting out in nature, or limiting screen time. Make a chart to help them "rate their day" for how they did with taking care of their body and brain for the day.

Hidden Rules: 1. Everyone feels better when they get enough sleep. 2. Drinking enough water and eating the right foods help your brain and body function at their best. 3. Exercise and stretching can improve your mood 4. Taking a break or having "alone time" can change your mood and make you feel better.

We can help children by co-regulating, which means that we stay calm and help them manage their feelings and adapt their behavior when needed. We can do this in many ways, such as using a calm tone of voice, getting down to their level, reducing the number of words we use, and also by validating and naming their feelings, such as, "I can see that you are upset; I understand, and I'm here for you."

—Leah Kuypers

SIBLINGS

What Do We Have in Common?

Help your children interview another family member and spend a day focusing on what they have in common to see if they can come up with as many commonalities as possible. Have them write these down and share them with the family so that they can be highlighted more often. For example: "How about if you both get bagels from the coffee shop that you both love so much?" or "Hey, I saw that the next *Star Wars* movie is coming out. Since you both love *Star Wars* so much, why don't we go as a family? Do you want to set up a calendar to count down the days together?" Highlighting similarities with siblings can provide perspective on what they have in common and increase bonding.

Job Talk: *"Do you want to be the interviewer?"*

What's Their Side?

When there is a conflict between siblings, help them discuss or write their interpretation of what happened. Make sure they include their feelings and use "I" statements, such as, "I felt left out and sad when you had your friend here and didn't let me play with you." Allow each of them a certain amount of time (e.g., two to three minutes) to express how they feel and take turns where one person is the "talker" and the other is the "listener." Have them repeat what they heard each other say and ask if it's correct. This activity should not be done in the heat of the moment. Make sure that the children are calm and able to share their thoughts and feelings in a respectful and safe manner.

▶ **To Expand:** Help the siblings make a cartoon about the disagreement with speech bubbles expressing each person's feelings to provide a visual representation and add a little levity.

Job Talk: *"Can you be the listener/talker?"*

Job Talk: *"Can you be the host/hostess?"*

Slumber Party

Take turns having each sibling plan, organize, and invite the other sibling to a slumber party in their room. Even if they share a room, they can practice being the host and come up with fun games, snacks, and activities for the slumber party. The idea is for the host to learn how to think about their sibling, and what they might want to do at a party (e.g., dance, eat popcorn, etc.). Maybe the host can come up with an art project or read a book to the sibling before they go to bed.

SIBLINGS

Swapping Responsibilities

From time to time, have your children swap chores and other responsibilities. For example, if one child usually takes care of the dog and the other takes care of the cat, have them swap those duties for a day or week. Other ideas would be to have them switch off making lunches for each other or picking out their clothes. Brushing each other's teeth might be taking it too far, but could be really funny and make them laugh. Swapping chores helps children learn to take the perspective of their siblings.

Yours, Mine, or Ours?

Have your children make a list of items in the house that belong to individuals (e.g., shoes, favorite stuffed animal). Make a list of things that belong to more than one person (e.g., car keys are for both mom and dad). Finally, make a list of what belongs to everyone (e.g., games, food in the fridge). Talk about which should be shared and how you would ask to borrow them. Role-play asking to share or borrow an item from another family member.

Job Talk: *"We can all be the sharers!"*

Job Talk: *"Is it your turn to be the complimenter?"*

Star of the Day

At least once per month, have each child be the "star of the day." Have the other sibling(s) think about all of the favorite things that the "star of the day" would like (e.g., food they like to eat, activities they might want to do, shows they might want to watch), and what they could say that would make them feel good (e.g., "I like that new outfit" or "It was fun watching you play soccer today.")

Rebooting

Introduce the concept of "rebooting" (or restarting) with your child when they are stuck on an idea about how things should be, or are inflexible about sharing, playing, or solving a problem. Encourage them to take a break and reboot. Just as a computer sometimes needs to reboot and start over, so do children.

Contributed by Rebecca Branstetter

Hidden Rules: 1. Having siblings is not always easy. 2. It is hard for parents to give their attention to all of their children at once. Sometimes, it might feel unfair, and that is okay. 3. It is okay to feel jealous of your sibling or get mad at them, but it's not okay to hit or say mean things to each other.

SCREEN TIME AND MEDIA MANIA

Where and When?

Create a family plan for where and when all members (including caregivers) can use their phone, tablet, or other devices in the home and community. This can be discussed as a group or family and put into a contract. Use visual reminders to show the places and times they are allowed and not allowed. The plan can include specific locations or screen-free zones (e.g., dinner table during meals) and screen-free times (e.g., M–F: no screens before homework and chores are done, and no screen time after 8:00 p.m.). These can be customized for an entire family or individualized for each member (e.g., a younger child may get less screen time than an older child, and parents may need to use screens for work or important communications that are different than playing games or watching videos). Templates for developing media plans can be found online at commonsensemedia.com. Set up a clear plan for screen time to help manage the time spent on screens.

Teach Me How to Play

If video games are allowed in your household, and your child is interested in playing them, have them teach you how to play a favorite game. Coach them how to give you the overview of the game, the objective for winning, specifics for how to play, and strategies. Children love being the teacher from time to time, and engaging in their interests can build connections between you and your child.

▶ **To Expand:** If there is a game that you like to play, invite them to learn from you as well.

Job Talk: *"I'd love to be the learner if you can be the teacher."*

Media Vacations

From time to time, plan a "vacation" from media and screens. This can be built into the weekly schedule (e.g., Saturday afternoons for four hours). Plan what the vacation will look like (e.g., going for a walk, cooking together, gardening, etc.). The media vacation can also include an outing. Too much screen time can overstimulate children's brains. Explain this to them and map it so they understand the need for breaks.

▶ **To Expand:** Have your child make a place in the house where no media is allowed (e.g., calming corner or playroom). Make sure there are lots of other fun things to do in this media vacation spot, such as books and games. Listening to books on audio is another fun way to spend time together without screens.

Be a Media Model

Our children learn how to regulate their media use by watching us. Model healthy habits by making sure you are not texting while driving or looking at a screen during a conversation with your child or other people. When you are at the park with your child, turn off your phone and play with them or model sitting and observing. Make sure you are following the family media plan that you set in place for your household, but it is also important for children to realize that their screen time rules may not apply to the adults at all times. However, dinner is a time when the whole family can shut down screens, including turning off the TV and having each family member put away their phone and focus on each other.

Hidden Rules: 1. Too much screen time is not good for your brain. 2. It is rude to look at your phone when you are talking to someone. 3. Phones, tablets, computers, TVs, and other screens are a privilege for children, not a right.

DAILY TRANSITIONS

HOME

One Step at a Time (First. . .Then)

Teach your child that things happen in sequence: "First this, then that." Provide encouragement for what they have trouble completing (e.g., "First, pick up your toys, then we can go for a walk."). You can also use the words "If . . . then . . ." (e.g., "If you get your homework done, then we can play a game.").

Job Talk: *"Can you be the starter?"*

Social Rules Change from Situation to Situation

Have your child notice how the people in the family react differently depending on the setting and the people involved. For example, the adults at home may sit close to each other but will not sit as close to visitors who come to your home or to strangers in public. Mom may speak in a loud voice to get someone's attention at home, but speak more quietly to get a clerk's attention in a store. Help your child make a list of the way that rules change depending on the setting or people involved.

▶ **To Expand:** Go to different locations, like the library or store, to make a list of what is different in these locations and what kind of behavior is expected there.

Job Talk: *"Be a social rule predictor."*

Toolbox of Calming Strategies

Use an old toolbox or a plastic bin to represent a "strategy toolbox" and fill it with "tools" (strategies) your child can use to help regulate emotions and solve problems during difficult transitions. Work together to come up with tools that might be effective in calming their emotions. This may include a favorite stuffed animal, pictures of things or people, fidgets to squeeze, or visuals of how to take a deep breath (See the Six Sides of Breathing visual on page 126). Remind your child that the toolbox is there to help whenever they experience big emotions or problems.

Contributed by Leah Kuypers

Transition Songs

As a family, come up with different songs that will be played to let your child know that it is time to transition to another activity or event. For example, have a song that alerts them that it is dinnertime, a song that conveys that it's bathtime, or a song for when it's time to leave the house. Pick songs that are more energetic for getting up in the morning and more calming for nighttime.

Hidden Rules: 1. Some people get uncomfortable when things change, but they try to act calm so others don't feel uncomfortable. 2. You can look around at the space and people to determine what is happening in the moment and what might be happening next. 3. Sometimes things change, even when they have been planned out.

IN THE COMMUNITY

IN THE CAR

Set the Child Up for Success–Priming

When you are in the car, discuss where you are going and what is expected of your child when you get there. Will they have to be quiet, or can they play and run around? If this is the first time at a given destination, explain who will be there and what will be happening. Should the child be focusing on one person (e.g., the birthday boy)? If you're visiting somebody's home, help your child think of things that person likes to talk about (e.g., what are the top three favorite things to do?). This kind of priming increases their level of confidence and helps them think about the person you are visiting and understand how to act, which can calm anxiety. It also helps children develop a mental picture and improve situational awareness for the future (forethought).

Debriefing

On the way home from an activity or outing, use the car ride to do some debriefing, or perform a social autopsy (see page 125) to figure out what did or didn't go well by reviewing and reflecting on what happened. Use these teachable moments to talk about what went well and what your child could do differently next time. For example, ask, "How do you think the birthday went? How do you think Sam felt when you gave him his birthday present? How do you think he felt when you put your finger in his cake without asking?" We can all learn from our mistakes and increase the ability to use hindsight. Discussion and reflection after social situations have occurred build insight and problem solving and can also be a celebration of a job well done.

▶ **To Expand:** Refer to the Mood Meter on page 112 both during and after the activity and check in about how your child is feeling. If you don't have the Mood Meter nearby, ask them to describe how the activity made them feel.

Job Talk: *"Can you be a comparer?"*

Same but Different

If you are going to a new place that is similar to places you have visited in the past (e.g., a new movie theater), use priming and help your child identify how the new place will be the same but different (e.g., the concession stand is smaller or the seats are different). This will help create a mental image of what to expect and be more flexible about the situation since it isn't the same as the movie theater that they usually go to. This may prevent possible behavioral outbursts caused by anxiety.

Be a Kind Commuter

When driving with your child, model kind gestures, such as allowing other drivers to merge, stopping for pedestrians, and calling for help if someone's car is not working. Make sure to discuss what is happening with your child so they are aware of your thoughtfulness and good driving etiquette. Make sure to not yell at other drivers, cut them off, or take a parking spot from someone else. We are models for our children, both in and out of the car.

IN THE CAR

What Can I Guess About Others?

Help your child make inferences and build awareness of nonverbal clues by paying attention to people in the street. Do they have a suit on? Gym clothes? Are they driving a mail truck? Help them read these social cues and make a logical guess about their vocation and where they might be going.

***Job Talk:** "Can you be the guesser?"*

Share Your Feelings

If there is a lot of traffic or you are running late, express your feelings of stress and tell your child how you are working on staying calm by using a tool that helps you (e.g., listening to classical music, using self-talk, taking deep breaths). Ask your child what they would do to keep calm and if they have any suggestions for you. It's important for their social emotional growth to see that we all work on keeping ourselves calm in stressful situations.

Social Lotto

Create a social lotto game to play in the car to build social awareness and inferencing skills. Find photos of people of a variety of ages and paste them on a sheet of paper. While you're in the car, have your child make guesses about places you pass where these people might like to go. For example, if you have a photo of a girl and you pass a toy store, see if your child can tell you why the girl would want to stop there.

STOP and Breathe

When you are in the car with your child and you come to a stop light or have to wait for construction on the street or a train to pass, practice doing some belly breathing by tracing the steering wheel on one side for breathing in and the other for breathing out. Turn down the music and have your child join in. Belly breathing is a tool for self-regulation. Using time in the car to model and practice with your child will help them prepare for stressful times in the future.

▶ **To Expand:** Put a circle, triangle, square, or hexagon on the back of the seat for your child to see from the backseat. Have them trace the lines of the shapes by breathing in and out (See Six Sides of Breathing on page 126).

Hidden Rules: 1. When you are in the car, it is important that you stay seated, keep your seat belt on, and keep your hands and feet to yourself. Do not distract the person who is driving. 2. When getting out of the car, it is safer to get out on the side close to the sidewalk. If you get out on the side with traffic, use caution when opening the door and getting out. 3. Keep your feet on the floor when you are sitting, and not on the seat in front of you. 4. Traffic can cause stress. When there is a lot of traffic, be sure to be quiet so the driver can focus on the road. 5. People don't like to have a dirty car, so always take your trash with you when you get out. Don't throw it out the window.

AT THE MALL

Why Are We Here?

Tell your child that you're going to the mall to play a game in which they will be a *social detective*. It's their job to try to figure out why you're going there or what you need to buy. Suggest that they ask Wonder Questions (See page 114) to determine your reason for going shopping and what you are going to buy (e.g., What size is it? Who is it for?). Observing social situations and making guesses using the information you know and observe are important parts of social competence. This game keeps children engaged and focused on the activity, and teaches how to problem solve and *follow the plan*, just as good shoppers always do.

Job Talk: *"Do you want to be the detective?"*

Asking for Help

Pretend you don't know where to find something in the store and ask your child to get help from the store clerk. Suggest getting the clerk's attention in an expected way (e.g., "Excuse me, may I ask you a question?") and to remember the response and to give back to you. Knowing how to ask for help and advocate for oneself is a valuable life skill that needs to be taught to all kids, but especially to those with social challenges.

▶ **To Expand:** If your child is shy or uncomfortable in this situation, start by making the requests for help very simple (e.g., "What time is it?"). Remembering directions is more difficult than remembering a simple one-word answer.

What's My Perspective?

Start by creating some simple thinking and emotion cards, using index cards and a marker. Write down one word or phrase on each card. Thinking cards might include: *That was nice! That was silly! I like that! I hate that! That's good! That's not so good.* Emotion cards might include *happy, sad, scared, mad, okay, frustrated*, etc. Match the thinking and emotion words to your child's social level. Use the cards when you're together in different situations to explore thoughts and feelings and the perspectives you each have (e.g., How are the perspectives similar? How are they different?). For instance, while you're at the mall, sit down and people-watch. Pick out someone wearing unique clothes or a group of guys who are acting goofy. Have them pick a thought or emotion card that reflects their perspective. Then you do the same. Talk about whether your perspectives were the same or different.

Contributed by Michelle Garcia Winner

AT THE MALL

COMMUNITY

"Do You See What I See?"

Find a place to sit and relax at the mall and ask your child to observe people who walk by or are sitting near you. Do they see someone who looks like they are going into a pet store? What could that mean? For example, the person might have a pet at home who needs food, or they might want to adopt a new pet. Compare your social observations to see if they are similar to your child's, and then talk about the importance of making guesses. When we're engaging with other people, we need to make observations and think about what they might be thinking. This can give us clues about what they might want to talk about. Don't forget to talk about the need for using discretion and not blurting out observations that others might hear.

***Job Talk:** "Can you be a people watcher?"*

Coping with Emotions

Use social briefing (e.g., prepare them for what is ahead) to help your child predict expected ways to cope with emotions that may arise at the mall (e.g., excitement, disappointment, hunger). For example, if it is close to dinnertime and you know they will want a cookie when smelling the aromas at the cookie store, explain that they can't have a cookie this time because it is too close to dinner. Having this conversation before the problem occurs helps children prepare for frustration.

▶ **To Expand:** Create a set of cue cards before outings that may be attached to your bag or belt on a key ring to display an emotion (e.g., disappointment) on one side and expected coping strategies on the reverse (e.g., we can take a photo or write down an item we cannot buy today, and then add it to your wish list.).

Contributed by Emily Rubin

***Job Talk:** "You can be a door holder."*

Hold the Door, Please

Have your child practice holding the door open for people when they walk in or out of a store. Encourage them to watch people's faces and see if they can tell how doing this kind gesture made them feel.

Hidden Rules: 1. Most stores don't allow you to bring food or drinks inside. 2. Calculate the change/money that you expect to get back before buying an item, so you don't take too much time at the register when it's your turn. 3. Always wear socks (either your own or the throwaway kind that some stores have) when trying on shoes, and underwear when trying on clothes (especially when trying on a bathing suit) in a store. 4. Make sure to give enough personal space to people when you are in public places. 5. Wash your hands before and after going to public places and consider wearing a mask if concerned about spreading germs.

AT THE PLAYGROUND OR PARK

Sharing is Caring

Have your child bring an extra toy, ball, or shovel to share with another child with whom they might want to play. Help them invite another child to play. For example:

"I have a ball. Do you want to play catch?"

"I'm making a castle. Do you want to build with me?"

Job Talk: *"Be the inviter."*

Who Should I Play With?

Practice observing other kids at the park with your child. Help them observe and find a child who might have the same interest as his (e.g., more physical such as playing with trucks or digging in the dirt versus quieter such as swinging on the swing alone).

Job Talk: *"Do you want to be the tagger/chaser/ thrower/runner?"*

Sharing Your Imagination

If there are clouds in the sky, lie down on the ground with your child. While looking at the sky, ask them to imagine that the clouds are animals or objects. Share your imagination with each other and compare what you see. Always encourage creativity and even "outlandish" imagination; your child may be the next great inventor!

▶ **To Expand:** If your child has a hard time coming up with an original answer, try giving the name of something you see and have them find it in the sky, such as "I see a cloud that looks like a duck!"

Partner and Group Activities

Tag, chase, and ball toss can be great fun for kids and build reciprocal play and interaction. When it's hot, fill squirt bottles with water to use in a game of tag. Another favorite is ice races, where children balance a piece of ice on a spoon and race across the grass. This can be done with one other person or in teams of kids. Take it slow with group games; they require a lot of social skills and flexibility. Note: your child might be sensitive to loud sounds or the way the water or ice feels on their skin. Sensory issues are important to consider when playing with others.

▶ **To Expand:** Sometimes it's a good idea to practice these kinds of group activities in pairs at home before trying them out with other people.

Hidden Rules: 1. It is important to always ask if you can play with someone else's toy. Sometimes they may say "No," and it is important to be calm if they do not want to share. 2. Don't throw anything (e.g., sand or rocks) at others. The exception is a ball, but only if you ask them first. 3. If you find toys at the park that are not yours, it is best to leave them in case someone comes back to look for them. 4. Wash and sanitize toys and hands before and after playing in public places.

AT THE GROCERY STORE

Grocery List

Have your child help make up the family grocery list. Go through the cupboard and refrigerator together, and ask them to guess what you need to buy at the store. To eliminate a list of candy and soda, use a typed list of standard items, and have them check off what is needed. This will help children develop planning and organizational skills. See sample grocery list on page 124.

▶ **To Expand:** If your child doesn't read yet, make a picture list to check off.

Job Talk: *"You be the list maker."*

What Aisle?

Make your child responsible for part of the grocery list. See if they can figure out where items are located in the store, based on the categories in each aisle and section. Provide prompting if needed, such as the indirect prompt, "If all the salad stuff is in the produce section over here, where do you think we can find the lettuce?"

Job Talk: *"Can you be the shopper?"*

What's Cooking?

When waiting in the line at the grocery store, take a look at what the people have in their cart and try to determine what they are making. If they have meat, BBQ sauce, corn on the cob, and potato salad, are they having a BBQ? If they have milk and cereal, are they planning ahead for breakfast? Encourage your child to observe their surroundings and make these types of logical guesses (i.e., inferencing) on a daily basis.

Hidden Rules: 1. It is a good idea to walk, not run, in the grocery store. Be careful not to block other people with your cart. 2. Wait to eat food until you have paid for it. You may get in trouble for tasting or eating food before it's purchased, unless it is a special tasting display. 3. Make sure to give enough personal space to people when walking in the aisles and standing in line. 4. Wash your hands before and after going to public places and consider wearing a mask if concerned about spreading germs.

EATING OUT

Step by Step

On the way to a restaurant, see if your child can sequence all the steps that are involved in eating dinner at a sit-down restaurant: 1. Pick the restaurant. 2. Get there. 3. Greet the host. 4. Wait for a table. 5. Sit down. 6. Order your food. 7. Wait for the food. 8. Eat. 9. Pay the bill. 10. Leave the restaurant. Mapping out the steps for an event is part of what is called "priming" which provides an understanding of what is going to happen.

▶ **To Expand:** If your child is a picky eater, help them plan ahead for what they might order and that they might need to be flexible if the restaurant doesn't have what they want. For example, they might have to order spaghetti instead of macaroni and cheese.

Master Chef for the Day

Help your child imagine what it would be like to be a chef and think about all the things that they would have to do to run a kitchen and make the food just the way everyone likes it. This is a great way to "step into someone's shoes" and take perspective. You can role-play this at home before going out to eat. You can also ask the manager of your favorite restaurant if your child can visit the kitchen to see what goes on there.

▶ **To Expand:** Have your child help you prepare a meal and be the "master chef," narrating all of the necessary steps as you do them.

Job Talk: *"Can you pretend you're the chef?"*

Job Talk: *"Be a social detective!"*

Social Secret Agent

Help your child observe others at a coffee shop or restaurant and try to determine what their relationship is to each other (e.g., mom and son, husband and wife, grandma and granddaughter). This is also an opportunity to help your child understand how to be discreet when observing, so they don't make others feel uncomfortable. Reading these types of social cues helps the child increase *social detective* skills.

What Are You Going to Have?

Look at the menu and ask your child to make a logical guess about what the people at your table or in your family will order based on what they know they like to eat. Model this by saying, "The last two times we were here, Dad got the chef salad. I bet he'll have that again because he talked about how much he likes it." Making logical guesses based on hindsight (past information) builds executive functioning skills.

Hidden Rules: 1. It is expected that you are patient and wait quietly while food is prepared and delivered to your table. 2. When you're finished eating, wait for others to finish before getting up to leave. 3. Stay off your phone and pay attention to the other people at the table when eating with others to make them feel comfortable. 4. Wash your hands before and after eating.

AT THE DOCTOR'S OFFICE

Easing Fears

If you suspect your child is nervous about going to the doctor, explain that this is a common feeling for people before going to the doctor. Validate their feelings and provide some calming tools that you know work (bring a favorite toy or book; do some deep breathing, etc.). Tell your child how you keep yourself calm when you go to the doctor. Validating feelings can reduce anxiety in stressful situations.

Do a Practice Run

Role-play and act out what it's like to go to the doctor. Practice sitting in a waiting room quietly and getting an exam. Reverse roles and have your child give you an exam to show that you have to visit the doctor sometimes too. Write a brief story or check out a book about going to the doctor for your child to read and review to prepare better for what to expect. Show photos of waiting rooms and doctors' offices to give a visual of what it will look like.

▶ **To Expand:** Purchase some common items that doctors use, such as tongue depressors, stethoscope, cotton balls, or alcohol pads. Practice with these items at home.

Job Talk: *"I'll be the patient and you be the doctor."*

Guessing Your Stats

Have your child make a logical guess about his height and weight based on what his statistics were the last time they were at the doctor's office. Making guesses based on hindsight (past information) is part of executive functioning.

▶ **To Expand:** Keep a record at home of the guesses and measurements from each time they go to the doctor so that they can reflect back on the accuracy and make comparisons.

Hidden Rules: 1. While waiting for the doctor in the examining room, it is important to be quiet and not touch the equipment that is on the counter or in the drawers. 2. It is unexpected to ask people in the waiting room why they are at the doctor's office or to tell them why you are there. 3. When sitting in the waiting room, leave one to two seats open between yourself and others to give enough personal space. 4. Wash your hands before and after your visit and wear a mask if you are sick or concerned about germs from others.

AT THE MOVIES

Preshow

While waiting for the movie to start, talk about what you already know about the movie and predict what you think it will be about. This builds perspective-taking and the ability to think ahead (forethought).

Movie Critic

When the movie is over, talk about what you liked or didn't like about it. Try to recall the events and help your child come up with three to four main points they can share with another family member or friend without giving away the whole plot. Rehearse before sharing to build confidence.

***Job Talk:** "You be a movie critic."*

***Job Talk:** "Be a whole-body listener."*

Quiet in the Theater

Review all of the steps for Whole Body Listening (See page 122) and discuss the importance of this type of listening in the movie theater (i.e., even though you're not talking to someone directly, you're sharing space with others who are trying to listen and watch the movie, too). Social rules are everywhere. Using real life situations can help your child learn these more readily.

The Spotlight's on You

Ask your child to pick a character from the movie and have them describe what they know about that person. Have your child step into the character's shoes and try to feel what it would be like to live that person's life. This is great for building perspective-taking and empathy.

Hidden Rules: 1. It is important that you are quiet and keep your feet and hands to yourself in the movie theater. 2. It is important not to tell others how the movie ends if they haven't seen it yet, unless they ask you. 3. It is okay to eat and drink at the movies, but do it quietly so it doesn't bother others. 4. Most theaters don't let you bring your own food. 5. When possible, sit several seats away from people you don't know in the theater to give expected personal space.

AROUND THE NEIGHBORHOOD

COMMUNITY

Exploring Your World

Have your child make a list of the things that they see on the way to school, the park, or around your neighborhood. Have them explore, observe, and gather information to share with the family. Did they notice that someone got a new mailbox or is preparing to paint their house? Did they see new flowers coming up or someone planting new bushes? Observing and sharing thoughts is an important part of relating to others.

Job Talk: *"Be an explorer!"*

Who Are the People in the Neighborhood?

On your walks, help your child make observations about the environment. If they see a house where there are toys on the front porch, do they think children live there? If seeing a cat on the prowl, does your child think a bird might be nearby? If there is a doghouse in the yard, do they think the neighbors have a dog?

Job Talk: *"Can you be a greeter?"*

Safety First: Don't Talk to Strangers

Talk to your child about who to talk to and who not to talk to. Friendly greetings are expected when you already know someone. However, when you don't know someone, it is not a good idea to talk to them. Going for a walk in the neighborhood is a good time to practice friendly behavior versus community awareness and safety.

▶ **To Expand:** Sit down with your child and make a list of who is and is not a safe person. For example, it is okay to talk to a police officer even if you don't know them, but not to a stranger who isn't wearing a safety uniform.

Neighborhood Niceties

Walk in your neighborhood and have your child practice greeting your neighbors with a warm smile, a friendly head nod, or a verbal "Hello." Maybe even have them ask how a neighbor's day was or how the dog is doing. A final "Nice to see you" is a great way to end greetings. If your child is not comfortable with this, model these behaviors while they observe.

▶ **To Expand:** If your child is shy or still uncomfortable with these behaviors even after you model them, try rehearsing or acting out these neighborhood niceties with puppets or stuffed animals before you go outside.

Hidden Rules: 1. It is important to watch for cars when crossing the street. 2. When taking a walk with someone, walk next to the person. 3. Move over to allow other people to pass on the sidewalk if they wish.

SPORTS EVENTS

Playing Ball

Playing sports offers lots of teachable moments. If your child has the skills and desire, have them participate in group sports and talk about the rules and what is expected. Practice what they will say if the child's team wins versus loses and talk about how the others might feel if they say something unsupportive. Provide a list with pictures of the rules for them to review when needed. Being a good sport and practicing sportsmanship can take lots of practice, but it's important for building teamwork and flexibility. It's also great exercise!

Job Talk: *"Can you be a spectator/ cheerleader?"*

Watching Sports

Taking your child to a sports event can be fun, but may also be challenging because of the logistics, including crowds. They may also have emotions about wanting their team to win. Turn such events into teachable moments. For example, even if someone is cheering for the other team, make supportive comments. Don't "talk trash" (i.e., speak poorly) or diminish other people's viewpoints.

▸ **To Expand:** Be a good role model and practice at home while watching sporting events on TV. Start by going to smaller sports venues with familiar people before attempting a larger crowd with strangers.

Building Emotional Vocabulary: A Sport in Itself!

Sporting events and intense emotions go hand in hand. Help your child build their emotional vocabulary and awareness by pointing out the various emotions players and fans are experiencing. Such emotions may include: *disappointed, upset, worried, motivated, competitive, elated, frustrated, confused, furious, ecstatic, exhausted*. You can also discuss whether an emotion was expected or unexpected given the circumstances. For example, if your team scores and the fans are cheering, that is expected; but if a fan from the opposite team yells bad words, that is taking it too far and considered unexpected.

Contributed by Leah Kuypers.

Hidden Rules: 1. When playing a game with someone, it is expected that you finish the game, even if you are losing. 2. Everyone wants to see the action. Don't block someone else's view. 3. If someone gets hurt in a sports game, show support by clapping when they get up or are assisted off the field.

GET OUT IN NATURE

COMMUNITY

Nature Hunt

Before going out for a walk or hike, make a list of various items to hunt or look for, such as a bird, a flower in bloom, a plant with thorns, or other things in your location. Observation and detective skills are building blocks for social and emotional awareness.

Job Talk: *"Let's be nature detectives!"*

Get Artsy

At a park, beach, or in your backyard, create art by collecting natural materials, then make a collage at home. Sticks, rocks, leaves, acorns, sand, and shells are all terrific art supplies. Your child can practice planning and sequencing by imagining the artwork and then gathering the needed materials.

Job Talk: *"Be a nature artist!"*

Find Your Green Thumb

Gardening is a great outdoor activity that can be done as a solo or group activity. Plan ahead and come up with the sequence of what needs to happen. First decide where to garden and what you and your child will plant. Whether you're growing flowers, herbs, or vegetables, teach what is required to make them grow (water, sunshine, care, etc.) and how they need to be cared for. Create a schedule so they will know when to water the seeds or plants. Your child will learn that it takes a lot of responsibility and nurturing to keep something alive, and it takes patience to watch it grow.

▶ **To Expand:** Visit a local nursery, garden, or farm to see an example of how other people help plants grow. Help make a list of the plants the child really likes, so that you can grow them at home.

Job Talk: *"Can you be a mindful listener?"*

Listening Walk

Take a mindful "listening walk" with your child in nature and have them try to focus on just the things that they hear. Listen for as many different sounds as you can. Try to identify the sounds (e.g., birds chirping, cars honking, dog barking, the wind). Bring a journal to write them down and then compare them with the other person's list. Mindfulness helps to train the brain to focus on one thing at a time, which research shows can help with self-regulation and impulse control.

▶ **To Expand:** Record the outdoor sounds with your phone or a tape recorder, then listen again at home to see if they notice anything different.

Hidden Rules: 1. When you go out in nature, it is a good idea to protect plants, animals, and insects, and not destroy them. 2. If you go on a hike, it is safe and respectful to always stay on the path. 3. It is a good idea to hike or walk with a partner or group of people, not alone.

HOLIDAYS AND SPECIAL EVENTS

GOVERNMENT AND NATIONAL HOLIDAYS

It Takes a Village

Help your child practice teamwork by explaining the concept that "It takes a village" and that people need to work together to keep communities running smoothly. Children can contribute to society and the welfare of others by working toward something they believe in. For example, if they care about the environment, have them be in charge of recycling at your house, make a recycling container for their classroom (with the teacher's permission), or write a letter to the newspaper on Earth Day about recycling.

Job Talk: *"Are you a recycler?"*

Model Citizen

To be a good citizen, you and other adults in your family can vote, obey the law, serve on a jury, volunteer, work toward change that you believe in, and be nice to others. By being a model citizen, you show your child what is important and how we work together for the greater good.

▶ **To Expand:** When there is an election, do a practice election at home. Make a ballot box and have everyone vote, either on the actual election issues or on issues in your house. You can also give your child a choice of volunteer opportunities, then volunteer at the site of his choice.

Job Talk: *"Do you want to be a voter or volunteer worker?"*

Crowds and Noisy Places

When going to a parade or somewhere noisy, talk to your child about how to manage the crowd and noise. Discuss and role-play how to keep their body in their own "space bubble" and how to not lean or push on people nearby. Let them know that touching others can make them feel uncomfortable. Bring earplugs, cotton balls, headphones, and/or a hooded sweatshirt to protect their ears from the noise of the crowds or possible fireworks. If your child becomes overwhelmed in crowds or noisy spaces, it can help to problem-solve and discuss this ahead of time.

▶ **To Expand:** Bring a Five Point Scale along to help your child identify when the crowds or noise are getting to be too much, so they can avoid being overloaded. One would be "Very calm," three could mean "Starting to get anxious," and five might mean "Too much! Get me out of here!"

Hidden Rules: 1. It is a good idea to talk about your views on some political topics only in certain settings. It's best to have these conversations with people with whom you are very familiar. 2. It's offensive to tell someone that they are wrong in their political or social beliefs.

MOTHER'S DAY/ FATHER'S DAY

Showing Love to Mom/Dad

Instead of buying a gift card or picking something out for your child to give, help them brainstorm what Mom or Dad might want as a gift for Mother's or Father's Day. Having children think about what they like and what makes them happy helps them to practice thinking about what others like.

Queen or King for the Day

As Mother's/Father's Day approaches, help your child prepare for making their mom/dad feel like a queen or king for the day. Help them make a card letting Mom or Dad know how much they appreciate them and all that they do. Help your child think of things they can do throughout the day that would make parents happy, such as getting them a cup of tea or bringing them breakfast in bed. Focusing on one person and what will make that person happy builds perspective-taking.

▶ **To Expand:** Your child can join with siblings to sing a song to Mom or Dad as a special gift.

Job Talk: *"You can be a bed maker/dog walker/dish washer."*

Happy Helpers

Parents and caregivers love when children help around the house, help with a younger child, or even just take care of themselves on their own. Help your child make a list of the things they can do to help and turn those things into coupons that they can give on Mother's or Father's Day. They can include chores such as taking out the garbage, walking the dog, folding the laundry, etc. See sample coupon on page 120 and a list of age-appropriate chores on page 134.

Hidden Rules: 1. Giving a gift that is homemade is a special treat. It is a "thinking of others" gesture. 2. Families come in different shapes and sizes. Some have two homes, some have two moms or two dads, and some have just one parent. It is important to be sensitive when talking about Mother's Day or Father's Day because some children don't have the same kind of mother or father. 3. It is important to remember that other people like things that you may not. It is kind to give things to others that they like, rather than things you like.

HALLOWEEN

Costume Detective

Look at people in costumes or photos of people in costumes and help your child determine how they feel and what they might say (e.g., how does the witch feel and what does she say?). Encourage them to use what they already know about the characters to make logical guesses about their feelings and how they express themselves.

Job Talk: *"Be a costume detective."*

Ghouls and Goblins

After your child has chosen what they want to be for Halloween, have them figure out what accessories that character might need and how they might act based on their knowledge of the character. Role-play how they will act when they are "in character" if they go to a party or go trick-or-treating.

▶ **To Expand:** Write a script or skit together for more structured practice in taking the perspective of the character. For example, create a skit in which the superhero character is startled by a monster decoration at someone's door. Practice having them respond as the superhero would.

Job Talk: *"Do you want to be the scooper? I'll be the carver."*

Pumpkins Can Show Feelings!

Carve pumpkins with various facial expressions. Have your child identify and act out how the pumpkins might be feeling and what they might say depending on how they look. You can also have them draw a facial expression on a pumpkin with markers as a template for you to cut. Encourage them to notice the expressions on the pumpkins compared to the expressions on real people. Discuss these expressions together to increase awareness of what they might mean.

Job Talk: *"You be the bag-holder/trick-or-treater."*

Trick-or-Treat

Role-play trick-or-treating with your child. Point out that it is a nice gesture when people give out candy and treats and that it is important to show appreciation by thanking them and treating them with respect. During the evening, take a break to rest and do a social autopsy about how the night is going, evaluating what is going well and what might not be going so well. Praise them for the things they are doing well, such as "I noticed you thanked the man who gave you that candy." If coaching is needed, use this time to do so, such as, "Let's try to keep up with everyone so that we can be part of the group." See page 125 for a sample social autopsy worksheet.

▶ **To Expand:** Refer to the Mood Meter on page 112 both during and after the activity, and check in about how your child is feeling. If you don't have the Mood Meter nearby, ask them to describe how the activity made them feel.

Hidden Rules: 1. If you say something mean about someone's costume (e.g., "I was that last year; that's for babies"), it will make them feel bad. 2. If offered a choice, take one piece of candy or treat from each house when trick-or-treating. 3. Trick-or-treating usually starts when the sun goes down and ends before 9:00 p.m. 4. If the light is not on at somebody's house, that usually means that they are not home or are not handing out candy, so don't knock or ring their doorbell.

THANKSGIVING

Giving Back

Make a family tradition of thinking about others who are less fortunate than you. Make a plan to visit a shelter, serve food to the homeless, or visit a nursing home to show that you care about others. Let your child choose how they would like to "give back" to others. This is a great opportunity for stepping into other people's shoes and being aware of and grateful for the things that you have.

▶ **To Expand:** If it is not possible to volunteer on Thanksgiving, plan a kind activity to do at home that day, such as writing holiday cards for service members overseas or drawing cheerful pictures for senior citizens in retirement homes. Your family can mail or deliver these the next day.

Job Talk: *"We can be givers!"*

Planning a Meal

Have your child help make part of the Thanksgiving dinner to build planning and sequencing skills. Include them in reviewing the recipe, buying the ingredients, and sequencing the steps involved in cooking the meal. Make sure that they are acknowledged for their hard work, perhaps in front of the family so that others can hear, (e.g., "I'm grateful for Miguel's help with preparing this special meal."). Positive experiences and praise build confidence.

▶ **To Expand:** Discuss the importance of indigenous people's culture and traditions and how we can honor them within this holiday.

Job Talk: *"You be the baker/chef."*

Sensing Your Senses

Help your child identify body sensations by talking about the way that the body feels while prepping and eating Thanksgiving dinner. How do their arm muscles feel when mashing the potatoes? How do their hands feel when washing them with warm water before the meal? How does your child's body feel when sitting in the chair at the table? How does their mouth feel when taking a bite of warm, sweet pie? Building awareness of how the body feels is a foundational skill for understanding emotions and building self-regulation. Use the Sensation Words on page 132 to help describe their observations.

Contributed by Kelly Mahler

Hidden Rules: 1. Families give thanks in different ways. Some pray, some hold hands, and some make a short speech. When someone at the table gives thanks, it is expected that you listen quietly (some people close their eyes and bow their head). 2. It is nice to help set the table and help clean when there is a large family gathering. 3. It is nice to say, "Thank you" to the person who did the cooking for the day.

OTHER MAJOR HOLIDAYS

Holiday Gift Giving

When thinking about what to buy people for the holidays, involve your child and have them look through magazines and make guesses about what each family member would like. If they have trouble thinking of a gift for somebody, have them interview the person to find out what they would like. Gift giving is great for perspective taking and learning to think of others.

Job Talk: *"Be a gift giver."*

Bigger than a Breadbox

Have your child make a guess about what's in a gift before opening it. If it is flat and square, could it be a book? Activities like this are great for inferencing and predicting.

Job Talk: *"You can be a guesser."*

Teaching the Skills

Discuss, explain, and role-play in preparation for the various events that will take place over the holidays. Some examples are: sitting at the dinner table during several courses, waiting for others to open gifts, etc. It is important for your child to "*add to the fun*" of the holidays instead of "*take away from the fun*." Knowing what is expected will help ensure that it happens.

▶ **To Expand:** Create a holiday calendar that includes holidays from other cultures to post on the refrigerator. Discuss, learn, and incorporate other traditions into your family.

Charity Begins at Home

Make a family tradition of thinking about others over the holidays. Donate a gift to a charity or give to someone in need. Giving and serving others builds compassion and empathy for others.

▶ **To Expand:** Do a Secret Giver project, in which each person is randomly assigned a family member or neighbor to secretly provide with small gifts or notes each day or week of the season. You can also "partner up" with one parent helping each child come up with ideas. Make sure to take into account each person's cultural or religious beliefs in thinking of gifts.

Hidden Rules: 1. Not everyone celebrates the same holidays. Remember to be sensitive to other people's culture and beliefs. 2. It is unexpected to tell somebody what you're giving them before they open the present. Be patient while others are opening their gifts so you don't spoil their enjoyment. 3. Holidays can be stressful for adults who have a lot of work to do to prepare, so try to be helpful or stay out of their way.

"Social relationships are the "fuel" for learning. As our children develop their confidence with engaging with others, their language, executive functioning and academic skills will also grow. The tools within this resource serve to empower children, and those who support them, with a foundation to build social connections, relationships and success in the real world."

—Emily Rubin

BIRTHDAY PARTIES

Shopping for Others

Have your child brainstorm about what the "birthday person" enjoys and likes. Go to the store while thinking of that person and pick out a gift that they would like. Have a conversation about the fact that what the birthday boy might like as a gift might be different than what your child or other children might like. This is a great activity for thinking of others and building perspective taking.

Job Talk: *"Be a thoughtful shopper!"*

Goodie Bags

Most children remember the last part of a social event the best. If they leave with a special treat or goodie bag, this helps create a positive memory about the party. Help your child decide what should go into the goodie bags at their party by thinking about what their friends enjoy and what those friends might like to take home.

▶ **To Expand:** Have your child make a personal party favor with a "Thank you for coming" card attached. Thoughtful gestures build empathy and connections.

Thoughtful Words

Help your child make a birthday card for a friend, keeping in mind what color their friend likes and what type of stickers they might like on the card. Help them write something nice or thank the person for the invitation to the birthday party.

BIRTHDAY PARTIES

Pretend Party

Role-play the events that typically occur at a birthday party (e.g., playing games, unwrapping presents, blowing out candles, eating cake) to prepare your child for each situation. Set up children for success by priming them ahead of time.

Birthday Letter to Yourself

Have your child write a letter to themself on their birthday that highlights things they would like to remember from the past year. Help them highlight the times spent with other children and how they have grown in various areas. Encourage them to think about the year to come and develop some areas on which they would like to focus (e.g., "I would like to have the neighbor kids over more" or "I want to find a club to join at school"). This type of reflection helps to build executive functioning by using hindsight and forethought.

▶ **To Expand:** Save these letters each year, and create a book full of them that your child can look at as they get older to get a sense of how they have grown.

Job Talk: *"You be the writer."*

Thinking About the Gift Giver

Teach your child how to do a "*social fake*" by having them practice keeping a neutral or happy face even when they don't like a gift that they were given. If they already have a particular item that someone gave them, encourage them to say "thank you," rather than "I already have that."

Hidden Rules: 1. It can make others uncomfortable to invite yourself to somebody's party or to complain if you are not invited. 2. Don't tell the birthday person what gift you bought. It's a surprise; let them wait to open the package to find out. 3. It is unexpected to unwrap others' presents or blow out the birthday candles unless you are asked to help. 4. The birthday boy or girl is in charge at the party. If you don't like the theme or are not having fun, keep those thoughts to yourself; this is the perfect time for a *social fake*.

DINNER PARTIES

Helping the Host

When you have a dinner party or barbeque at your house, assign your child a role or "job" for helping out. Have them set the table, greet the guests, take photos, or clean up before or after the party. Help them to complete the assigned task by providing prompts or supports and don't forget to provide encouragement along the way. Offering a "job" or something to do at a gathering can help your child get involved and builds leadership skills.

▶ **To Expand:** Ask if your child wants to pick the assignment. When they are helping at the event, help them think about what the guests might be thinking.

Job Talk: *"You be the greeter/photog-rapher/cleaner/ dish washer, etc."*

Party Tricks

Have your child think of something to share with guests, such as reciting a poem, playing a tune on the piano, recalling facts or stats from history or a sports game, or showing them the new sports or magic trick that they learned when people come over. This can be a nice way to entertain guests at a party. Practice ahead of time and pick a special time for the performance. See sample kid tricks on page 127. Ice breakers are a simple way to initiate conversation in social situations.

Job Talk: *"Be a singer/joker/pianist."*

Act It Out

Let your child know what is expected during a particular gathering (e.g., being quiet at the table, playing quietly). Take time to act it out and practice what is expected before the guests come, especially if they have a "job" or "assignment" to help with. Set realistic expectations and rules and make sure they are clearly understood.

Hidden Rules: 1. When guests come to your house, it is expected that you say "Hello" and ask them to come in. 2. It's thoughtful to compliment and say "Thank you" to the host for inviting you before you leave. 3. Ask to be excused from the dinner table before getting up.

VACATION PLANNING AND ORGANIZATION

Itinerary, Please!

Make sure to map out what's going to happen on your vacation for your child. A schedule of the entire vacation plan is good so that all family members know what is expected. In addition, a schedule of the daily events can help them know what is happening throughout the day, and can reduce anxiety stemming from unfamiliar experiences, people, and transitions. A social narrative can be written and read prior to the vacation to set them up for success. Photos or drawings can also be used for a narrative. Children benefit from knowing what the plan is for the day, especially on vacation.

Tour Guide

When you arrive at your vacation destination, have your child be the guide by reading the map, picking up brochures, and pointing out the different sites to see.

▶ **To Expand:** Use a map to show your child where you're going, how long it will take, and when you'll be taking rest breaks. Let them have their own map so they can help be the navigator, marking off places you have visited.

Job Talk: *"Can you be the navigator?"*

Job Talk: *"You be a planner."*

Sticking to a Schedule

Although vacations typically don't follow a set routine, try to develop some sort of daily schedule to help your child understand, predict, and expect when it's time to eat, sleep, etc. If the schedule will change for a day, communicate that to them, and have your child help develop the new plan. Don't forget that healthy eating and sleep can help every child be a happy camper. Routines and schedules provide predictability and reduce anxiety for your child.

Hidden Rules: 1. When riding on a plane, keep your body to yourself. You're sharing a very small space, so only use one armrest, even if other people use more than one. 2. Not everyone likes the same music. When you're in the car with other people, be flexible and listen to what others like to hear as well as what you like. 3. Sometimes airplanes are late. Try to wait calmly and keep yourself occupied with a book, game, or music during the wait.

VACATION FUN

How Are They Connected?

If you're sitting by the pool, hanging out at the beach, or waiting for an airplane, play *social detective* games with your child, such as "Guess who belongs to whom." Watch people around you and try to decide who is related and belongs in the same family. For example, if two children are playing together and sitting with their parents, they are probably brother and sister. This type of guessing helps build observation skills for understanding social situations and relationships.

Job Talk: *"You be the detective/observer."*

Special Memories

Have your child write or draw in a journal about the high and low points of the vacation, helping as needed. They can also write a story to share with friends when you return. Drawing or writing in a journal can help them process feelings and reflect on their experiences.

▶ **To Expand:** Refer to the Mood Meter (See page 112) both during and after the activity and check in about how your child is feeling. If you don't have the Mood Meter nearby, ask your child to describe how the activity made them feel.

Job Talk: *"Be a journalist."*

Job Talk: *"Can you be the story reteller?"*

Document and Tell Stories

Be sure to take photos to document your trip. When you get back, put them in an album and review them with your child. Practice telling brief stories that they can share the experience with other people. This is great for conversation starters after a vacation.

VACATION FUN

"Say Cheese!"

Take pictures of the people on your trip who are displaying various emotions. Help them determine how the person is feeling based on their facial expression and body language. Vacations are a good time to do some people watching and build awareness of emotions and nonverbal clues.

Job Talk: *"I'll be the photographer and you be the smiler."*

New Places, New People

When you visit a new city or country, teach your child about the culture, living conditions, or way of life of the people who live there. Help them think about others and realize that other people live different lives than their own. This builds perspective taking.

▶ **To Expand:** Before you leave on your trip, prepare some fun facts about the destination that your child can learn and share with family members.

"Name that Tune" and Other Car Games

Play "Name that Tune." Have each person give clues about the song about to be sung, including the name of the singer, the style of music, what show it is from, and the number of notes you are allowed before you guess.

▶ **To Expand:** When going on family car vacations, be sure to bring other car games, such as Bingo or 20 Questions.

Hidden Rules: 1. Most of the friends you make on a short vacation will only be friends for that period of time. 2. Put your bathing suit on before you go to the pool to swim and always wear sunscreen. 3. When on public transportation, it is expected that you use a quiet voice when talking. 4. At the pool, don't make comments aloud about other people's bodies. 5. Go to the bathroom before you get in the pool; it is unsanitary to pee in the pool. 6. There are chemicals in the pool that are not good for you to drink. Try not to swallow the water in which you are swimming.

BRIDGING HOME AND SCHOOL

This section is meant to provide suggestions to parents and caregivers about how to prepare your child for school and how to best support and partner with teachers and school staff. It includes suggestions for how to prepare your child for the school day, how to help with homework, and how to practice the social, emotional, executive functioning, and academic skills needed to be successful at school.

SCHOOL DAYS-PLANNING AHEAD

What Do You Need?

With help from your child's teacher, create a calendar with activities that are happening at school for the upcoming week, such as group projects, library day, or a school assembly. After putting the activities on a calendar, review them with your child the day before to discuss how they might need to prepare. Do they need to bring something for the group project? Return a library book? Think ahead for what will make your child comfortable for the assembly? Preparing and priming children will help their success with these activities.

▶ **To Expand:** You can make a copy of the calendar for your child's binder or backpack so that they have a visual to refer to during the day.

Proactive Feel-Good Breaks

Come up with a menu of activities that feel good to your child, such as stretching, doing yoga poses, drinking water, getting fresh air, going for a walk, talking to someone they trust, playing a game, etc. Practice these activities at home and develop a few that they can do throughout the school day on a regular basis, after first checking with their teacher about how and when these might be used. Teach your child that these activities are not just for when they feel stressed or need to calm down. They can be used proactively to help with daily body awareness and emotional regulation.

Contributed by Kelly Mahler

Job Talk: *"Be a visualizer!"*

Visualize the Day Ahead

Help your child plan ahead and visualize their day by first writing the activities (e.g., getting ready, going to school, going to music class, coming home) and then closing their eyes to picture doing these activities in sequence. Can they picture being in these places? What are they doing? How are they feeling? Is there anything needed to bring along to prepare for the day?

Hidden Rules: 1. A calendar, planner, or schedule can help you know what is coming next and plan for the future. 2. Thinking about what is coming next can also help you plan ahead. 3. When moving your body or stretching, make sure that you are not touching or bothering the people around you.

GETTING READY FOR SCHOOL

Match the Picture

To build executive functioning and help your child visualize a mental image of what to look like to get out the door for school, take a picture of your child dressed and ready to go to school with everything needed. The next day, show the picture to help them get ready. Explain that this is what it looks like when they are ready: fully dressed with shoes, hair and teeth brushed, backpack on, etc. Tell your child to "Match the picture."

Contributed by Sarah Ward

Prepped and Ready

Mornings are often rushed and hectic; this can be frustrating for everyone. As part of the nightly routine, have your child help pick what they want for lunch the next day and what they want to wear, and put their "ready" backpack by the door for a smooth transition to school the next day.

▶ **To Expand:** Make a visual schedule for this routine so that they know what is expected and can *follow the plan*. Have them do as much as they can on their own to get motivated, build independence, and get organized.

Watching the Clock

Help your child understand how to manage his time by explaining what is involved with getting to school on time. Start by saying what time they need to be at school. Then map out everything they have to do to get ready for school (e.g., get dressed, eat breakfast, feed the dog, etc.) and how long each of those things take to get done. Explain how long it takes to get from home to school, then add up all of the time. Help determine together what time your child needs to wake up to do all of those things and get to school without being tardy. If you are using a visual schedule for the morning activities, add a visual of a clock that shows the times for each activity.

▶ **To Expand:** Use a visual timer on your phone or other device to help your child "see" the time passing. Provide them with a watch to help them take responsibility for regulating and planning their time throughout the day.

Special "Love Notes"

Write a sweet note to your child and put it in their lunchbox or backpack for them to read when they are at school. You can include notes like, "I'm thinking about you," "I'm proud of you," "You are special," "You rock," or "I hope you are having a great day." Other ideas are drawing a picture or including a silly cartoon to make them laugh or maybe share with a classmate to start a conversation.

Hidden Rules: 1. It is a good idea to wear warm clothes when the weather is cold and lighter clothes when it is hot. 2. If you don't get enough sleep, you might be drowsy at school. It's hard to participate and focus in class when you are tired. 3. Eating healthy food is good for your brain and body.

HOMEWORK TIME

Grand Central Station

Create a Grand Central Station for anything that your child needs for school and homework. This could be a corner of their room with a cubby or a desk or a central area where the family does their work. Teach your child to keep this area organized so they can find what is needed (e.g., backpack on the same hook, pencils in a box, paper available, etc.). This will prevent these items from getting lost or scattered around the house.

Contributed by Rebecca Branstetter

Job Talk: *"Let's be organizers."*

Backpack and Binder Prepper

Have your child empty their backpack on a weekly basis to organize and remove anything that is not needed (e.g., old papers, food, dirty clothes, water bottles, etc.). Make sure they have the materials needed for the coming week and that everything has been turned in that was completed. Take the time to help organize the binder, too.

▶ **To Expand:** Color-code any folders for each class or subject to make them easy to find when needed for a specific class.

Job Talk: *"Let's both be workers!"*

Homework Schedule

Set up your child for success by setting a specific time and schedule for homework. Provide short breaks for them to walk around or do something that helps regain focus when needed. Consistently provide support and praise, and do something relaxing or fun with them after they are done. Consider doing your own work (e.g., reading, paying bills, or other focused work) next to them while they do homework.

Places and Spaces

Help your child find a comfortable and conducive place to do homework by determining the best place for them to focus. Do they feel more comfortable alone in a room? Or is it better to be around others who can help and provide support? What type of lighting is best? Is background noise a distraction? Help your child determine this by discussing the options and how each choice feels. Experimenting including trial and error might provide helpful insight.

▶ **To Expand:** Help your child come up with and create a sign that lets others know they are hard at work and trying to concentrate. This visual may also help your child remember what they should be doing and regulate their own behavior.

Hidden Rules: 1. Each school and teacher assigns homework in different ways. 2. Homework usually increases as you get older. 3. Everyone has different strategies that help them focus and get their work done.

A "WHOLE-CHILD" TEAM APPROACH

Informational Letters

Informational letters to the teacher about your child can provide valuable information to set up both your child and the teacher for success. These one to two-page letters or outlines can include facts about the child, strengths, areas of need, any allergies, temperament, medications, diagnoses, triggers, sensory needs, language needs, physical needs, tips/strategies, outside support/therapy, and goals. See page 136 for a sample letter.

Build Rapport

Good rapport with your child's teacher often builds bridges for a strong partnership with the home and school. Take time to get to know your child's teacher. Volunteer in the classroom, ask what supplies are needed, or bring gifts or cards. Putting in this effort often goes a long way. You can both learn from each other to better support your child's needs.

Job Talk: *"Can you be a meeter and greeter?"*

Orientation, Please

Take the time to show your child around the school, classroom, therapy room, etc., before starting a new school year, class, program, or therapy. Introduce any new teachers or support staff when possible and explain who they are and their purpose for supporting your child. Providing an orientation or doing a trial run can often reduce anxiety and build confidence for new situations or transitions.

HOME/SCHOOL

Hidden Rules: 1. Teachers have a lot of students to keep track of and get to know. They work long hours before and after the school day. 2. Teachers have their own families and lives outside of school. Sometimes you will see them in an unexpected place in the community, like the store. It's okay to say "Hi" to them if you see them outside of school. 3. Ask your teacher if it's okay to ask about their personal life or what they did on the weekend.

SUCCESSFUL SCHOOL DAYS

Schedules and Routines

Develop predictable daily routines, especially around times that might be more challenging for your child, such as starting the week or day, transitioning to or from school, or doing a task they don't enjoy. Make a visual schedule with the steps involved to build structure and awareness of what is expected of your child and to decrease verbal redirections. For example, help take photos of what is needed to get out the door in the morning (e.g., getting dressed, eating breakfast, brushing teeth, getting backpack ready, etc.) or find simple pictures online. Print the photos and develop a visual schedule from top to bottom or left to right for your child to use when it is time for that specific activity.

▶ **To Expand:** Changes in the schedule will happen. Discuss this with your child and role-play how to manage a change in the schedule. Make a visual icon to represent "Change," such as the word paired with a bright color.

Make it Visual

Many children are visual learners and struggle to understand or remember information presented to them orally. You may see things in your child's classroom that provide visual structure for both children and adults, such as photographs, visual schedules, seating charts, Venn diagrams, infographics, graphic organizers, hand signals, labels, drawings, etc. Ask your child's teacher if any of these might help your child at home. Offer to help your child's teacher by creating these visual aids for the classroom and also make them for your home.

Celebrate Strengths

Research shows that children benefit from specific, sincere, and generous praise that celebrates effort and builds confidence. Ask your child's teacher to write a list of the positive things your child has done each week so that you can support the classroom by rewarding your child for these things at home. Some examples might be keeping his desk organized, lining up smoothly, or helping a peer.

Processing Time

If your child struggles with a lot of verbal information/teaching, ask the teacher for suggestions on how to help your child with this at home. Share that you are trying to be clear and concise when providing information at home and that you would also like to help your child remember important information from school.

▶ **To Expand:** Using a visual cue along with the verbal instructions is also helpful for many children.

SUCCESSFUL SCHOOL DAYS

Soothing Spaces

Let your child's teacher know what type of sensory input or modifications you use at home for your child. Share the lighting, auditory, olfactory, and tactile factors that affect your child and whether they are over or under-sensitive to this stimulation. Provide a list of the strategies you use at home, such as dimming the lights, providing headphones or seating options, reducing noise, or adding or taking away fans. See if the two of you can brainstorm ways to help the child feel comfortable and regulated at home as well as at school.

Job Talk: *"Can you be a counter?"*

Count Down

Teach your child how to count breaths when having to wait for something. Practice at home by role-playing how to do this for school situations, such as waiting in line for the bus, lining up for recess, waiting for others to be finished with an assignment, etc. If your child doesn't want to count breaths or their belly going in and out, ask if they would prefer to count fingers and toes, objects nearby, or shapes or colors seen in the environment.

Smooth Transitions

Ask the teacher if you can share the visual schedule that you are using with your child at home and ask if there is anything that might be incorporated for school success. If needed, offer to help make visual supports for your child and the classroom that might help with transitions for your child and others. Follow the teacher's guidance on what kind of visuals or schedules would be useful. For example, offer to help take photos of the classroom tasks or activities (e.g., cleaning up, lining up, going to lunch/eating lunch) or to print out pictures and develop a visual schedule from top to bottom or left to right for the students to use when it is time for that specific activity.

▶ **To Expand:** Ask the teacher if it would be helpful for you to provide a "supply pack" that might include Velcro, magnets, markers, or a white board.

Contribution from Rebecca Branstetter

HOME/SCHOOL

Hidden Rules: 1. Visual schedules and reminders can be taken to recess, on a field trip, or home to build independence. 2. If you didn't hear what the teacher said or don't understand the instructions, raise your hand to ask a question. 3. If you sit close to the window, door, or fan, it might be distracting and hard to focus on what the teacher is teaching.

PRE-GAME PRACTICE FOR RECESS

Time to Regulate!

Encourage your child to use recess for running around, playing physical games, swinging, jumping, going on the monkey bars, and getting some exercise. Help them become aware of how their body feels with the physical movement and exercise and how good it is for the body and brain for regulation. Explain what regulation means and encourage them to be a "regulator" to be more independent with learning coping and self-regulation skills.

▶ **To Expand:** Help children develop a routine for their time outside of the school room and teach how to invite other kids to join in. Let the teachers know how much you value recess and physical activity as part of your child's school day.

Job Talk: *"Can you be a regulator?"*

Be a Helicopter

Come to school early or stay later to help your child observe a social scene with other children who are playing and interacting with each other. Help your child imagine being a helicopter circling over a social situation. Ask them to look and listen for clues about how others are acting and interacting. Are they having fun? Do they look happy? Is it time to clean up? How can they tell? Observation skills are an essential part of social-emotional learning.

Job Talk: *"Let's be observers."*

Friendship Bench

Volunteer to decorate a bench or area on the playground at your child's school that children can sit on when they are feeling left out. It can be a place that students sit to show that they want to be asked to play or hang out with another child. Offer to help train students on how to use the bench.

The Power of Play

Teach your child how to play various recess games by teaching them the rules and what is expected of them. If they do not like to play physical games, encourage them to do alternative group activities, such as chalk art, gardening, or an indoor option such as board games or construction toys. Unstructured and facilitated playtime is just as important as structured academic time for a child's development.

Hidden Rules: 1. Recess equipment such as a swing, monkey bars, or digging in the sand can be a good tool to make your body feel relaxed. 2. Watching before jumping into play in a large group game can help determine what is going on and how to join in. 3. Many schools have an art, game, or library room open during recess for alternative choices to physical games.

SCHOOLWIDE KINDNESS

Pay It Forward

Help your child build empathy and perspective taking skills by starting a kindness campaign, in which the children "pay it forward" by doing nice things or volunteering to help out around the school (e.g., delivering items to classrooms, cleaning up at a school event, letting someone go first, giving someone a compliment, smiling or saying hello to someone, including someone new in the group or game, asking students from other classes to play, showing a new student around, giving a gift to the teacher, janitor, or receptionist, etc.). Have your child ask for permission from the teacher and get input. You can have your child make and print out "kindness bucks" to give to other students who do a good deed for someone else.

Learning Buddies

Ask your child's teacher if the school has a peer mentor program or buddy system. If not, offer to help develop a program where students are paired together to monitor and help each other out with academics, social skills, or other support that might be needed. Participants can be older and younger kids paired together or they can be students of the same age. Students are often paired together when one child needs extra help and the other has stronger skills to provide that support. Buddies can build social interactions, provide leadership opportunities, and also support anti-bullying.

It's Raining Kindness!

When the weather is rainy or snowy and the children are not allowed to go outside for playtime, help your child write or draw letters or cards or paint pictures to give to the other kids in the class to cheer them up. Talk about how this made others feel. Use the Mood Meter to check-in with your child during this activity (See page 112).

Job Talk: *"We are all going to be greeters."*

One-Minute Hellos

Teach your child how to greet others and start a conversation by saying "Hello" by greeting friends with eye contact or by using gestures, such as a handshake, high-five, hug or head nod, and, of course, a smile.

▶ **To Expand:** Don't forget to teach goodbye gestures, as well, and not leave classmates hanging.

Hidden Rules: 1. If you smile at someone and they don't smile back, they probably didn't see you smile at them. Try not to take it personally. 2. There are many ways to say "Hello" and give friendship greetings.

FIELD TRIPS, ASSEMBLES AND SPECIAL EVENTS

Plan, Practice, Proceed, and Review

When your child's teacher is preparing for exciting changes in the school day, such as an assembly or field trip, make sure to find out the plan ahead of time to prepare your child for what is expected. Review the step-by-step schedule and practice these steps, along with the rules, as needed. Proceed with the activities and review how things went after they are finished.

▶ **To Expand:** Show photos or videos of the event to provide a visual of what it will look like.

Making Connections to the Curriculum

When your child is going on a field trip or assembly, ask how you can support, extend, and connect what they are learning in the class. Is there new vocabulary that you can teach and use, or any explanations or conversation that you can have at home to help deepen the learning and experience?

▶ **To Expand:** Show your child pictures or research the location or topic that will be experienced ahead of time at the library or on the internet.

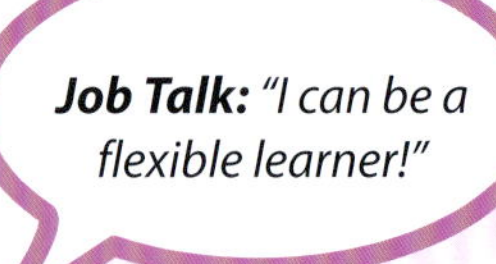

Be Prepared. . . for Change!

Field trips, assemblies, or out-of-the-ordinary school events require flexibility that can be difficult for many children. Before the outing or schedule change, talk about what it means to be flexible when things don't go as planned, such as needing to wait in line or not getting what you want (e.g., getting to ride in your friend's car). Role-play how to handle these situations and provide some language to build self-talk, such as "Everything will be okay" and "I can be flexible."

Hidden Rules: Field trips support learning through experiences. 2. Special school events and field trips take a lot of planning from all adults involved. 3. Most schools have field trips and assemblies a few times a year.

Children sometimes get frustrated with unexpected changes in their daily schedule. Parents might find themselves responding to the behavior as oppositional, rather than recognizing "flexible thinking" as a skill and teaching it in a systematic way. If you can think about this as a cognitive issue, rather than a "behavioral" issue, you can teach valuable coping strategies that will benefit your child throughout their life.

—Kari Dunn Buron

VOLUNTEERING AND GETTING INVOLVED

Contributed by Ruth Prystash

Coffee Club

Start a coffee club for other parents and help your child build social connections with classmates by building relationships with other parents in the class. These relationships can form the foundation for setting up play dates and party invitations. Secure an available room from the school administration or select a café off-site. Parents can contribute coffee and snacks or simply get together to share experiences and chat.

▶ **To Expand:** If you are a shy person or don't like socializing in large groups, just start by inviting one other parent to meet for coffee. Every relationship you build may help your child build relationships too, and you may also get new ideas from other parents.

Childcare Exchange

Parents often get burned out from the demands of daily life and could use a break but struggle with finding reliable or affordable childcare. Build relationships with other parents in your child's class by offering to provide them with a night of childcare. You can eventually start trading childcare services, so that everyone benefits. Use these childcare opportunities to foster relationships between your child and their classmates.

Sibling Support

Sometimes siblings of children who struggle with social, behavioral, or academic issues are overlooked. Ask your children's school about starting a sibling support group, such as the Sibshop program. Offer to get information about groups and volunteer to help get a group started.

Busy Parents Can Help Too!

Parents who work outside the home and have busy schedules often lack the time for conventional volunteer opportunities. Many teachers spend their evenings or weekends making materials—laminating, cutting, assembling packets, etc. Ask your child's teacher if there is something you can do at home in the evenings to help out. Even if you can't be at the school on a regular basis, your child will notice your interest and so will your child's teacher. You can do simple projects while watching TV or while sitting next to your child doing homework.

VOLUNTEERING AND GETTING INVOLVED

Volunteer Extraordinaire

Becoming involved in your child's school can help build relationships with the staff. There are many ways to volunteer; look for opportunities that suit your individual interests or strengths. You might teach sign language to your child's class, read stories in the school library, work at school carnivals, provide snacks for Back to School or Open House nights, prepare materials for teachers, chaperone field trips, or help with the PTA.

Play Date Host

Sometimes your child may need help in establishing friendships. You can help by hosting play dates at your house with one or two classmates. Have some structured activities, such as board games, craft projects, or cooking activities. Also allow time for unstructured play once the kids start to interact. These play dates can translate into more interactions at school.

Resourceful Resource Finder

Compile a list of community resources for parents in your area. These can include after-school sports or recreation programs, doctors or dentists who specialize in working with children with special needs, legal resources, free activities for families, summer camps, advocates, speech or occupational therapists, mental health resources, and anything else that might be helpful. You can print these out and give them to other parents, or you can give them to the school to hand out to families.

Hidden Rules (for parents): 1. Volunteering is a great way to make friends and build a community for you, your family, and your child. 2. All schools need volunteers to make things run smoother. 3. You can provide support during or after school hours for all kinds of events (e.g., raising money, helping with events, working in the classroom, going on field trips). 4. Volunteering and working with teachers and the school is a good way to model collaboration for your child. 5. Everyone needs support sometimes, including parents, siblings, and school personnel.

RECAPPING THE SCHOOL DAY

Daily Communication

Use a notebook, journal, or online program, such as a Google document, to communicate with your child's teacher. Let them know anything that happened at home after school, in the evening, or in the morning before they started their school day. This provides the teachers and educators with information that helps them understand how to support your child.

▶ **To Expand:** Let your child write in it as well. Maybe they want to tell their teacher a story about what happened at home or how they are feeling. They can even write a little thank-you note to the teacher.

Highlights of the School Day

When you have a chance to check-in with your child after the school day, ask them to highlight the best part of the day. If a visual is needed, use the 5-point scale on page 119 to map the gradation of best versus worst part of your child's day to help explain. For example, the best is a 5, something more neutral is a 3, and the worst part is a 1.

▶ **To Expand:** Help your child draw or write a story about this highlight of the day in a journal or a single piece of paper to post to see and review. Refer back to this reflection and help your child create positive thoughts about the school day so it's possible to look forward to similar situations.

Job Talk: *"You are a problem solver!"*

Challenge of the Day

On the way home from school, ask your child to share something that was new or challenging and discuss how they handled it. Ask about your child's feelings during and after the situation. Share something from *your* day that was difficult. Describe how you felt before and after this difficult situation. Explain that these are learning situations and that, although they might be uncomfortable in the moment, they can be celebrated as times that help us grow and learn. This type of conversation helps your child build a growth mindset.

Hidden Rules: 1. Parents do things during the day when you are at school, and it makes them feel good when you ask them about their day. 2. Talking about something that was hard or stressful about your day can help relieve pressure. 3. Everyone has ups and downs in their day. Sharing these can be a way of building connections with your family and friends.

The school-home connection is incredibly important. Collaboration between educators and families provides a child, not only with a balanced, consistent, and successful approach, but also with a sense of security, knowing that everyone is on the same team.

—Ruth Prystash

PART THREE

STRATEGIES AND TIPS

Don't Stop Now . . .

As a parent, caregiver, or educator, you have countless opportunities to teach and model social communication, self-regulation, and executive function. Daily life is filled with situations and activities that have many teachable moments—moments when we take advantage of everyday, natural opportunities to provide coaching, practice, and participation. This is actually a research-based method that encourages the learning and teaching of new skills in the home, school, and community, because these moments are happening every day in real time (Lowry, 2017). When we acknowledge and embrace teachable moments, we reinforce learning. Children can "walk the walk" and build social and emotional awareness related to real situations.

The hope is that the material and information in this book will encourage you to make the most of these moments, whether you are reinforcing behavior or helping a child practice a skill or rehearse for an upcoming event. Modify the activities in ways that make sense for the setting and the child's learning style. You are the best judge of what works in navigating a path toward social success for your child.

As you review the various activities, you'll likely recognize things you're already doing. Even if you haven't put a name to the strategies, you already understand many of the ways in which a child needs guidance. Take a moment to recognize all that you're already doing to support your child's development and continue to create more opportunities to help them thrive! In this section, you will find more information about the skills in the book and additional strategies that can help you be more effective in implementing them.

Strategies: Specific Ways to Provide Support at Home

As parents and educators, we aren't given an instruction book on how to teach our children. We rely on our instincts and past experiences. However, sometimes it is helpful to learn specific strategies that can make our own teaching more successful. Here are fourteen strategies that are especially useful when teaching social-emotional skills.

1. The Importance of Meeting Basic Needs

First and foremost, we cannot overlook the importance of keeping the brain at an optimal level of functioning, regulated, and primed for learning by making sure children get enough sleep, hydration, proper nutrition, and exercise. Without enough sleep, kids cannot think clearly or regulate their level of alertness or emotions and their behavior may reflect an inability to make desired choices. Food is our body's fuel, and water helps to regulate us. If a child is not getting these needs met, they will also struggle with processing information and regulating themselves. Make sure children get enough healthy protein and fat, and drink plenty of water each day.

Exercise is not only good for the body and for controlling weight, but it has also been shown to stimulate cognitive performance, help with focus and attention, and improve mood. There are fun ways to get more daily physical exercise, such as walking to school (or getting dropped off a few blocks away and then walking), playing tag, jumping on a trampoline (small ones can be indoors), walking a dog, having a dance party, or playing other indoor movement games. Just as plants need water to grow and thrive, children need the proper ingredients to fuel their brain function and set them up for a healthy social and emotional life.

2. Sensory Needs

Many children who struggle with social emotional learning are also impacted by sensory issues. These issues stem from over or under-responsiveness to stimuli that affect our eight senses. As described in Part One, these senses are sight, smell, hearing, touch, taste, proprioception (the ability to feel our body even if we can't see it), vestibular (movement and balance), and interoception (awareness of internal sensations, such as hunger or sleepiness). When children are negatively affected by input that is either too much or not enough, their skills and behavior suffer. It is critical for us to be aware of how the child is processing sensory information in their environment and make modifications when needed. For example, if we know that they get overstimulated by noise and lights, it's important to limit the time spent at an arcade or to avoid it altogether.

As social emotional coaches for our children, we can teach them to identify their sensory needs and utilize strategies to address them. These strategies can be as simple as dimming bright lights, wearing headphones, keeping a water bottle handy, or taking short movement breaks during the day. Sometimes, we must be sensory detectives to help our children figure out how they are being affected by their environment. Then we need to teach them to notice the warning signs of being too excited, hungry, tired, upset, or anxious that often indicate that sensory issues are at work. Be proactive at helping your child figure out their needs. Give children the vocabulary to describe their needs, and help them come up with a menu of environmental or physical changes that they can make to help themselves be more regulated.

3. Teach Mindfulness

Mindfulness is the ability to pay attention—on purpose, in the moment, without judgment (Kabat-Zinn, 2015). It's being able to "be in the moment" and be aware of your sensations, feelings, thoughts, and what is going on around you. It can create the ability to pause and understand how you, the situation at hand, and what reaction would have the best outcome. This skill is extremely important for SEL, in that it supports the ability to recognize emotions in yourself and others (emotional awareness), what is going on around you (social awareness), and how to act or what to do moment-by-moment (behavior/executive functioning). Mindfulness has also been shown to improve attention/focus, empathy/perspective taking, reduce anxiety/stress, and improve sleep (Weare, 2012).

As stated in Part One, there are many ways to practice this yourself and to teach it to children. It doesn't have to be about going to a weekend retreat, taking a yoga class, or sitting in silence for long periods of time. It can be going for a mindful walk without your phone or other distractions or noticing your feet on the ground or wind on your face. It can be sitting with your tea or coffee and feeling the warmth on your hands, smelling the aroma, and tasting each sip one by one, in a mindful, non-distracted manner. There are many books (See makesociallearningstick.com/book-recommendations) and apps for parents and children to explore. Try it yourself or learn and practice along with your child as part of the foundational ways to build SEL.

4. Follow the Child's Strengths and Interests

As parents and educators, we talk a lot about the areas with which our children struggle, and we often focus on the skills that are delayed. Although this is important to be aware of, it can be overwhelming for parents and certainly for the child. Imagine if the people in your world continuously focused on your greatest weaknesses. All of us, including our children, have strengths that can be highlighted and built on to help improve other areas of lagging skills.

On top of building on a child's strengths, it is also powerful to determine and focus on their interests. Some children have many different interests while others have less obvious ones or ones that are difficult to identify. Children learn best when they are engaged in activities that are highly motivating to them. For example, if a child is working on challenging math skills and they love blocks, it is a powerful strategy to use blocks in the process of teaching math skills. See page129 for a sample interest inventory.

5. Modeling

Most children see and hear more than we give them credit for. They often imitate what they see and hear and either purposefully or accidentally learn by observing the behaviors of parents, siblings, peers, and teachers. This is why it is important to model behaviors that we want children to learn (National Autism Center, 2011). Children notice how their parents and teachers treat others and they pick up on the language and behavior that we use and that they see in the media.

We can also be role models during play times. For example, if you lose a board game, say something like, "It's hard to lose, but I will try to be a good sport and not get upset; it was fun anyway." Also, it's good for children to hear positive self-talk so they can value the importance of internal encouragement and motivation. Show them that we all need an inner cheerleader to help us through life's hurdles. For example, when cooking say something like, "The last time I made these cookies, they were too dry. I'll put in less flour to see if I can make them taste better this time."

And remember, nobody is perfect. When you put your foot in your mouth or your child sees you behave in a way that you regret, take the opportunity to use that as a teachable moment. Show how to repair the situation, apologize, or do it differently. Use your own relationships, friendships, and social situations as a positive model for the child's social learning and development.

6. Priming

We all feel more comfortable when we know what to expect or what we are supposed to do during a specific task or situation. Where are we going? How long will it last? Who will be there? What am I supposed to bring or do when I'm there? These are common questions for everybody. It is important to recognize that children do better and are less anxious when they have an idea about what will happen in a given social situation. This knowledge will help set them up for success; they'll feel more at ease which may also reduce challenging behaviors.

Previewing information or activities that may prove challenging before an event happens is called "priming" (Aspy & Grossman, 2011; Koegel et al., 2003). It may be done by using a social narrative (Gray, 2000), a personalized story that describes a social situation (See page 128). It may also be used to show desirable behavior or to explain that something new often includes hidden social rules. This is an example of making the abstract more concrete. For example, "When you go to Johnny's house, his parents would like everyone to take off their shoes so the carpet doesn't get dirty."

7. Social Debriefing/Social Autopsy

Just as it's important to talk about what will happen in advance, it's also useful to talk about what happened after the situation or event occurred. Discussing outcomes and debriefing what went well and what could be done differently is often instructive. Also referred to as a social autopsy (Lavoie, 2005), this involves reviewing and dissecting how a social situation went after it has happened. With guidance, the child can analyze and examine social interactions and behaviors that contributed to a desired or undesired outcome. A social autopsy works best when the child is calm and focused. Review what happened and what went well, discuss what could have been done better, talk about alternative choices, and problem solve for the future.

Identifying particular behaviors and their outcomes make it more likely that the child will understand that it's something they either want to repeat or else do differently another time. Social narratives, words, pictures, or cartoons may be used to help the child reflect on what has happened.

This is also an excellent opportunity to practice considering and discussing how the other person might have felt (positively or negatively) in response to the child's actions, thereby building perspective-taking skills. This can be as simple as identifying and talking about how another person felt in response to the child's actions.

8. Teach Hidden Rules and Situational Awareness

Hidden rules, as described in Part One, are the unspoken rules that guide our social behavior. These are things that most children learn by observing others as they grow up. How to stand in line at the store, where to sit in a theater, or how to behave in an office or library—all are examples of rules that children learn by observing their parents, peers, and other people. And these rules are everywhere, in every setting, with every new situation. They help us understand what to say and how to act in various places, such as the library, movies, or at the dinner table. They involve understanding metaphors, idioms, jokes, slang, and assumptions.

Many children with social challenges are often very concrete thinkers, seeing the world in terms of black and white, and they struggle to understand the abstract social and emotional world. They develop a limited set of social rules in their minds and are often oblivious to the more subtle or hidden cues, as well as the context of a given situation. Their lack of situational awareness and difficulty with abstract thinking affect their ability to learn these hidden social rules. "Context blindness" is a term that is used for those who struggle to grasp the context of the situation. Unfortunately, many children with these challenges lack an awareness of other people's behavior, so they don't naturally "tune in" to how others are behaving, putting them at a real disadvantage or possibly even in danger. Many activities in this book provide opportunities to build awareness of the situation, context, and hidden rules, providing you with tips and tools on how to coach your child on these skills.

9. Role-Play and Rehearsal

Role-play and rehearsal (a part of role-play) give children an opportunity to act out real-life situations to problem-solve, practice social skills, and build an image of what something might look or feel like when it actually happens (Sohn & Crayson, 2005). For example, a parent or teacher could say, "Let's pretend you're at recess and someone bumps into you . . .", then act out what the child can do with their words, body, and behavior to manage the social situation. This provides an opportunity to find out how the child perceives various social situations and talk about how they feel going into a situation. The child can also gain insight into what others are thinking and feeling.

This type of practice can help with understanding and reading nonverbal cues, as well as thinking of what to say and not to say in a situation. Role-play can be used for practice working in a group, joining in play, having a conversation, or prepping for a job interview as the child gets older. By thinking about the situation and acting it out, various options can be developed and practiced to build self-esteem and confidence and promote positive social behaviors.

10. Play

Play is one of the most important ways children learn to be social. Play fosters language skills, sensory and motor skills, imagination, problem solving and planning skills, thinking about others, critical thinking, and social regulation. It offers an avenue for parents and caregivers to engage and connect with their children and provides teachable moments for skill-building and growth. Facilitating opportunities for play with other children supports developmental growth (Wolfberg, 2009). Play can take place anywhere and at any time, either during structured or unstructured time. Try to engage your child by following their lead and wishes with regard to the type of play and sequence of activities (Greenspan, Wieder, & Simons, 2008). Focus on the shared enjoyment of the moment rather than the product or outcome.

11. Scaffold and Prompt

Prompting and scaffolding involves giving children support, cues, or assistance to complete a task, learn something new, or achieve a goal. Just as construction workers build scaffolds to climb higher, we can provide assistance and guidance to children to help them gain skills and become more independent. There are various ways to provide this support, such as physical (helping the child build a tower by using your hand over theirs to pick up blocks and stack them); modeling (showing what to do); verbal (directly or indirectly stating what you would like the child to do, such as "Say hello" (direct verbal) or "What do you need to say when you see someone?" (indirect verbal); gestural (pointing or showing with your body/eyes what you would like the child to do); and visual (showing the child exactly what you would like them to do by modeling, using photos, schedules, writing, or other visual cues).

It is important to provide enough support to help the child be successful and feel confident but not do things for a child or provide too much prompting, so that they can build skills and eventually act on their own without assistance. For example, when providing support via indirect prompting, the child has to problem-solve and figure out what is needed on their own (e.g., "Hmm, I see unwashed dishes on the table") versus when we give them direct prompts and tell them what to do (e.g., "Please get your dish and put it in the dishwasher).

12. Visual Supports

Children listen to adults speaking to them all day, giving verbal directions, teaching/lecturing, or providing insight. This verbal instruction can become routine, causing children to tune out or possibly become irritated. Adding or substituting visual supports can increase focus, interest, responsiveness, and independence.

Learning styles vary, but using visual supports can help most learners. Supports may include photos, pictures, drawings, icons, objects, or written words. A visual schedule, map, scale, script, and photos help children know what is expected of them. These tools keep them feeling comfortable and able to follow a given plan. Providing this type of information helps to create a mental image, makes the abstract more concrete, provides structure, helps with transition, and reduces anxiety and frustration. Visual supports are also transferable. A child can take the visuals from one place to another and refer to them when needed. Even if the adults change from situation to situation, the visual instructions or prompts will remain the same, providing consistency for the child.

Social emotional learning is full of abstract concepts that are extremely difficult to understand, teach, and talk about. Presenting information visually offers a useful way to map out what people might be thinking or saying, provide organization, communicate what will be coming up next, and help make sense of social and emotional information, including hidden rules.

13. Reinforcement and Praise

We continuously tell kids how to do things or what not to do. It is also important to pay attention to what they're doing well and to provide feedback during those specific moments. Catch the child trying hard at something or being helpful or nice to others. Acknowledge the child's positive behavior by praising them with specific words or gestures that in most cases will validate the child and increase their drive to repeat these desired behaviors.

When verbally praising a child, acknowledge effort, hard work, and willingness to try (e.g., "I can see you're taking your time decorating that cake; it looks great" or "Wow, you didn't give up!"). This supports a growth mindset (Dweck, 2006) and intrinsic motivation to feel good about doing your best job. The opposite occurs when praising the child's natural abilities, such as intelligence (e.g., "You're so smart"); this creates a fixed mindset and can result in children not focusing on hard work and getting stuck if they think something might be too difficult.

Taking this strategy a step further, Sarah Ward, a speech-language pathologist and expert in executive functioning, recommends praising the action and outcome and then adding an exclamation to increase the child's awareness of the future and reason for the task. For example, rather than using global statements such as "Good job," which doesn't help the child understand why the task was important, say "Wow, thanks for hanging up your towel (action). Now it can dry on the rack (outcome). Cool (exclamation)!"

When we provide positive nonverbal praise or reinforcers for positive behavior, such as a hug or wink, desired behaviors will be nurtured and grow. This type of feedback can increase motivation and self-confidence. It can also help the child understand what it feels like to be successful, and will build a positive social memory tied to that desired behavior, thus increasing the motivation to perform the behavior again.

14. Job Talk

As mentioned in Part One, job talk is a strategy developed by Ward and Jacobsen (2012) in which a task or action is turned into a job and noun label. This change in phrasing from a verb ("greet") to a noun ("greeter") can significantly increase interest in the action and, in turn, transform a request into a positive action that implies independence and self-determination versus just being told what to do. Children show increased motivation to complete a task with "er" added to action words. That is, turning a task or action into a "job" and adding "er" gives the child a job title, such as washer, wiper, tooth brusher, listener, etc.

Manipulating the verb form of a behavior ("Annie, brush your teeth, please") to feature a noun label ("Annie is a tooth brusher!") creates a part of one's identity. It boosts confidence and a positive sense of self—"this is what I can do!" This subtle shift in language can change a child who engages in an occasional behavior of helping around the house ("Please set the table") into a child who has confidence in their permanent trait or skill ("I am a table setter."). Below are some examples.

Action/Verb Form	Noun/"Job Talk" Form
Wash your hands.	Can you be a hand-washer?
Please wipe the counter.	Be a counter wiper.
It's time to go upstairs and brush your teeth.	Time to be a tooth brusher!
Please take out your homework and start your math.	You're getting ready to be a mathematician.

15. Teach the Thinking Behind the Skills

Social emotional skills rely not only on how we perform an action, but also on how we think about being social and how we think about the people with whom we are interacting. These concepts are complex, resting on a variety of different pieces of information. What do we know about them? What are their beliefs, culture, and feelings? What do we know about the place or social situation at hand? How do we learn about the social rules at a new school or job? What do we say and how do we act to keep the people around us feeling comfortable? Not only are these skills abstract and difficult, but just when we think we have a social situation figured out, it may change. To develop an understanding of these skills, we not only have to teach the social skills (the behavior), but we also must talk about the thinking that comes *before* or goes with those skills.

This is what Michelle Garcia Winner refers to as **Social Thinking®**. The teaching framework she developed helps children become better social thinkers and social problem solvers. Her approach provides them with the tools and strategies to better understand their social surroundings and make good choices about which skills to use in the moment. Social thinking also involves developing a sense of how their behavior affects the thoughts of others, how others treat them, and in turn, how they feel about themselves (Winner, 2005). The idea of taking another's perspective may seem natural to those of us with neurotypical social development, but explaining this complex concept to individuals with social learning challenges can be difficult. To turn this abstract concept into teachable elements, Winner developed the **Four Steps of Perspective Taking**. These steps demonstrate that taking perspective is an active process that involves considering our own, as well as others' thoughts and feelings within the context of the situation.

The Four Steps of Perspective Taking (Winner, 2007)

1. When you come into my space, I have a little thought about you and you have a little thought about me.
2. I think about your intentions and you think about mine. Why are you near me? What do you want from me? Is it because you are just sharing space, do you intend to talk to me, or do you intend to harm me?
3. I realize you are having thoughts about me, and you realize I am having thoughts about you. We each think about what the other might be thinking.
4. I monitor and possibly modify my behavior to keep you thinking about me the way I want you to think about me. You do the same toward me. The thoughts we are having about each other are

often tiny thoughts that are almost at the unconscious level. However, it is this always-present, very active thought process about the people around us that allows us to constantly regulate our behavior to make sure most people have "comfortable" thoughts about us most of the time.

Many of the terms used in this book are part of the Social Thinking vocabulary developed by Michelle Garcia Winner. They provide a common language that adults can use with children to describe the abstract concepts that are part and parcel of everyday social situations or concepts that we often have a hard time explaining. For more information on Michelle Garcia Winner's Social Thinking program, go to www.socialthinking.com.

Social competencies are very different from social skills. Social skills are the output of a behavior. Social competencies are much deeper and require the mind to socially attend, interpret and problem solve in order to decide if, when and how we should respond. When we think socially our one mind considers many minds at once.

—Michelle G. Winner

A Final Word: Pulling it All Together

Although those of us who support neurodiverse learners have come a long way, we still have further to go. Social emotional learning is vast and complex! All of the pieces tie together and have an effect on the eventual success of a child. **Self-regulation** plays a huge part in **social communication** and vice versa because people constantly interact and share space. If a child is struggling with sensory input, feeling emotionally overwhelmed or cut off, or lacking executive functioning skills (impulse control, attention, initiation, etc.), it will be difficult for that child to be socially successful. And as parents and educators know, it's often the social situation with its variation and unpredictability, that causes a person to become dysregulated and less successful. This is why I often refer to it as social regulation, the combination of self-regulation and social communication, as mentioned in Part One.

It is through our support of children's social regulation that they will be better equipped to navigate the ever-changing social situations in which they will find themselves. Use the activities provided in this book, capitalize on the many teachable moments that daily life provides, and regularly practice these tools. By following these steps, you will be able to nurture the complex social, emotional, and executive functioning skills necessary for your child to develop stronger social regulation, thereby improving their interactions at home, at school, and in life.

As you embark upon this social emotional learning journey, it is important to remember that you are not alone. It really does take a village of parents, caregivers, educators, and friends to support the whole child. And now, along with the countless parents whose children need support with social regulation, you have this book and all of its activities and suggestions to help you better understand SEL, cultivate more hope from all the tools you now have, and feel both inspired and confident in your capacity to make social and emotional skills stick and contribute to your child's lifelong success.

You've read the book ...

Ready for the next step to create ease and confidence in your parenting skills?

Want to reduce your child's (and your) anxiety and overwhelm?

• • •

Want to move from big feelings running your home life to daily ease and joy?

• • •

Want to boost your child's emotional intelligence and social skills?

• • •

Check out:
MakeSocialLearningStick.com/freetraining

Take a step to get the support and community you need to grow your skills as a parent and support your child in their development

APPENDIX

The following pages are supplemental visuals and resources to support the activities throughout the book. For FREE downloadable color PDFs, hop on over to MakeSocialLearningStick.com/bookbonus.

Vocabulary

Vocabulary designated by *italics* throughout the book is part of the Social Thinking Vocabulary developed by Michelle G. Winner, www.socialthinking.com. Used with permission.

Adding to the Fun/Taking Away From the Fun: Adding to the fun is doing anything that encourages children to play together and have a good time. Taking away from the fun is doing things that might make others feel bad or not want to play together.

Doing What Is "Expected": Understanding that a range of rules (stated or unstated—"hidden") exists in every situation and that we are responsible for figuring out what those rules are, and then following them by adapting our words or behavior. By doing what is expected, we keep other people thinking good thoughts about us. Using the terms "expected/unexpected," rather than "good/bad" or "right/wrong," we remove subjectivity and demonstrate that what is "good" in one situation may be "bad" in another.

Doing What Is "Unexpected": Failing to follow the set of social rules, hidden or stated, in the environment. When you do what is unexpected, people may have confused/unfriendly/grumpy/mad thoughts about you.

Flexible Thinking/Flexible Brain: Using mental flexibility to interpret verbal and nonverbal information based on different points of view or different contexts. Being able to "go with the flow" and "see the shades of gray." This is the opposite of having a rigid or "rock brain," where one follows a rule all the time or gets stuck on one's own ideas or desires.

Following the Plan/Following the Group Plan: Understanding that, when in the presence of others, we work together to accomplish a common goal with all members thinking about the same plan. This involves taking into consideration what people are planning to do next based on their physical actions. We can also start to figure out what people are planning to do by interpreting the subtle meanings of their language. This is a higher-level skill.

Interruptosaurus: A silly name for someone who interrupts when others are talking.

Keeping Your Brain and Body in the Group: To participate effectively within a group, our brains need to keep thinking about what the group is thinking (a topic, an action, a lesson, etc.) and our bodies (eyes, head, shoulders) need to be situated in a manner that shows we are interested and connected to the group.

Perspective Taking: Understanding that other people have thoughts, feelings, beliefs, or experiences that might be different from ours.

Plan B: A second choice or plan for when unexpected situations occur.

Sharing Imagination: Being able to share your thoughts and ideas that you think about and imagine with another person. This is a large part of play and conversation.

***Smart Guess*:** Taking information you already know or have been taught and making an educated guess about something using that information.

Social Autopsy/Social Debriefing: Talking about or dissecting a social situation after it's done (Lavoie, 2005). This helps to understand what happened and determine what went well and what could be done differently next time.

Social Briefing/Priming: Explaining and outlining what is going to happen during an upcoming event or social situation. This helps prepare the child for what to expect.

***Social Detective*:** Looking at and thinking about the situation and the people in context. This includes using your eyes, ears, and brain to look for clues in the situation (the context) and from people to help determine what their plan might be or what they are thinking about.

***Social Fake*:** Demonstrating interest in someone else's topic even if you don't find it all that fascinating. We use the social fake during boring moments to keep people feeling good about being around us. This requires focused and friendly facial expressions, eye contact, supportive words and gestures, etc.

***Space Invader*:** Someone who gets too close to or invades another person's personal space. This shows the person is not thinking about others and what makes them feel comfortable/uncomfortable.

***Thinking With Your Eyes*:** Using your eyes to interpret a situation and the nonverbal messages others are sending as well as to show others you are thinking about them.

Whole Body Listening (Truesdale, 1990): This concept teaches that listening is not just hearing with your ears but using your eyes (to look at the speaker), mouth (stay quiet), hands (calm), feet (quiet on floor), body (facing the speaker), brain (to think about what is being said), and heart (to care about what the person is saying).

***Social Wonder*:** Thinking about what other people are interested in or how they feel and asking questions to gain more information from them about their interests, experiences, and thoughts.

Words Bumping: Another way to tell someone that they are interrupting.

Mood Groups

How are you feeling today?

Place the following visual with different facial expressions/feelings on the refrigerator or a central location for the child and family to view. Have the child reference this visual on a daily basis to help determine how he or she is feeling and what mood he or she is in. Encourage the child to share those feelings and talk about why he or she is feeling that way. Be a model and do the same by telling the child how you are feeling and why.

Sample Conversation Cards

Tell me about the most fun part of your day today.	**What did you see or do at recess today?**
What do you think the party will be like this weekend?	**Tell me what your most favorite meal is.**
What is happening in your art class this week?	**Who would you spend time with this weekend if you could pick three people?**
If you could go anywhere on vacation, where would you go?	**Tell me about the most boring or difficult part of your day today.**
Tell me about the book you were reading in class today.	**What is something you are excited about tomorrow?**

Other ways to start open-ended questions include

1. Tell me what happened.
2. Why did you …?
3. How did you …?
4. What do you think?
5. Why do you think that happened?
6. Can you think of another way to think about that?
7. What can you tell me about …?
8. How did you do that?
9. Does that remind you of something else?
10. What do you think might happen next?

Wonder Questions

Use this visual to help the child come up with questions to ask other people. This can prompt the child to generate a question that keeps a conversation going and shows others that he or she is thinking about them.

Typical Dinner Schedule

Make dinner.	Set table.	Sit down, eat, and talk.	Clear table.	Clean up.
	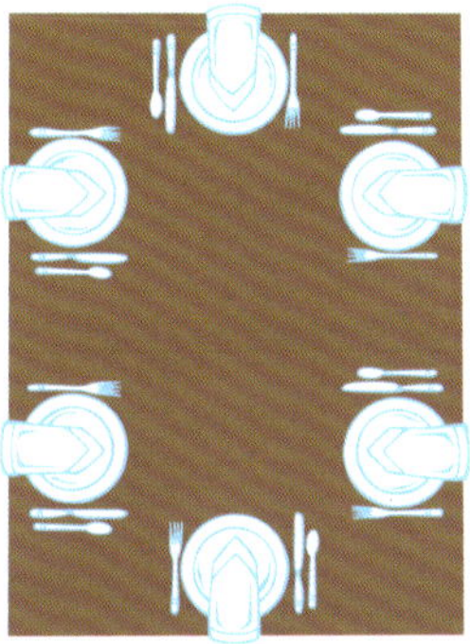			

Get Ready, Do, Done

1. Start with a picture of what a food item looks like when prepared and ready to eat (e.g., what does a ham sandwich look like when done?).
2. Figure out what steps you need to take to match the picture (DO).
3. What ingredients are needed to make the sandwich? (GET READY).

Now gather the ingredients, do the steps and when you are finished, look at it to make sure it matches the picture or what you hoped it would look like.

Eat it! (DONE). Great for building executive functioning skills!

Get Ready	Do	Done
What do I need? ☐ Ham ☐ Bread ☐ Cheese ☐ Lettuce ☐ Mayonnaise ☐ Knife ☐ Plate ☐ Other: ______ ______ ______	List the steps: Steps: 1. Get a plate. 2. Place two slices of bread on plate. 3. Use knife to spread mayo on one slice of bread. 4. Put cheese, lettuce, and ham on the same piece of bread. 5. Place other slice of bread on top of ham. 6. Cut sandwich in half. 7. Enjoy!	Before starting, determine what the final product will look like.
1. Look at the Done picture. 2. List all ingredients or materials needed.	List what is needed to do with the ingredients or materials to complete the finished product/goal.	Compare your finished product with the original picture or idea. Does it match?

Source: Sarah Ward, M.S., CCC/SLP, and Kristen Jacobsen, M.S., CCC/SLP (in press, 2014). Used with permission.

Visual Schedule to Transition to Play Time

From *Peer Play and the Autism Spectrum: The Art of Guiding Children's Socialization and Imagination* by P. Wolfberg, 2003, Shawnee Mission, KS: AAPC Publishing, p. 68. Used with permission.

Sample Kid Jokes

Q: What did the triangle say to the circle?
A: You're so pointless.

Q: What did Bacon say to Tomato?
A: Lettuce get together!

Q: What do you call a sleeping bull?
A: A bulldozer!

Q: What do polar bears eat for lunch?
A: Ice berg-ers!

Q: How many skunks does it take to stink up a house?
A: A phew!

Q: Why do witches fly on brooms?
A: Because vacuum cleaners are too heavy!

Q: Which dog keeps the best time?
A: A watch dog.

Q: What do you call a snowman with a sun tan?
A: A puddle.

Q: What's black and white and makes a lot of noise?
A: A zebra with a drumkit.

Knock, knock!
Who's there?
Cash!
Cash who?
No thanks, but I'd like some peanuts!

Knock, knock!
Who's there?
Ken.
Ken who?
Ken I come in? It's freezing out here.

Sample Puns

- Time flies like an arrow. Fruit flies like a banana.
- I've been to the dentist many times so I know the drill.
- Without geometry, life is pointless.
- I went to a seafood disco last week .... and pulled a mussel.
- She had a photographic memory but never developed it.
- To write with a broken pencil is pointless.

5-Point Scale for Nighttime Routine

Based on *The Incredible 5-Point Scale* by K. D. Buron and M. Curtis, 2012, Shawnee Mission, KS: AAPC Publishing. Used with permission.

I Am Thankful Worksheet

Use the following format to help the child write things that he or she is thankful for. If writing is a challenge, have the child dictate to you or use photos or drawings. This can be done before bed, at the dinner table, or some other time when you have the child's attention. Helping the child be aware of the people and things that he or she is thankful for builds awareness of the good in life and creates positive thoughts. Post the sheet on the refrigerator to remind the child of the good in his or her life.

I am thankful for:	*Because:*
1. ______________________	______________________
2. ______________________	______________________
3. ______________________	______________________
4. ______________________	______________________
5. ______________________	______________________

Just for you!

This coupon is good for:

____

Thinking about you,

____

Steps for Brushing Teeth

1. **Get toothbrush and toothpaste.**	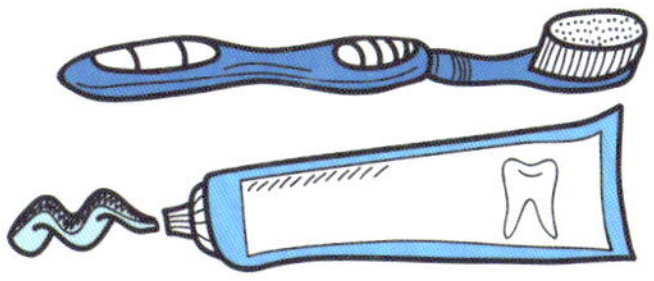
2. **Wet the toothbrush with water.**	
3. **Put toothpaste on toothbrush.**	
4. **Brush your teeth, each section (e.g., top & bottom, front & back, inside & outside) for at least 10 seconds, spitting toothpaste out as needed.**	
5. **Brush tongue.**	
6. **Rinse mouth with water.**	
7. **Put toothbrush and toothpaste away.**	

Whole Body Listening Handout and Coloring Sheet

1. Eyes = look at the person talking to you
2. Ears = both ears ready to hear
3. Mouth = quiet – no talking, humming, or making sounds
4. Hands = quiet in lap, pockets, or by your side
5. Feet = quiet on the floor
6. Body = faces the speaker
7. Brain = thinking about what is being said
8. Heart = caring about what the other person is saying

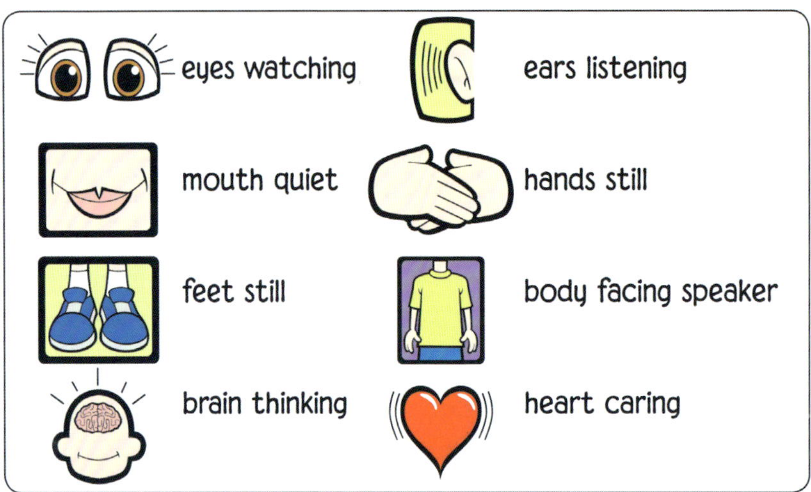

Whole body listening is a concept originally created by Susanne Poulette Truesdale in 1990. It was adapted and used by Sautter and Wilson in *Whole Body Listening Larry at School* and *Whole Body Listening Larry at Home*, 2011, San Jose, CA: Social Thinking Publishing. Used with permission.

Whole body listening is a concept originally created by Susanne Poulette Truesdale in 1990. It was adapted and used by Sautter and Wilson in *Whole Body Listening Larry at School* and *Whole Body Listening Larry at Home*, 2011, San Jose, CA: Social Thinking Publishing. Used with permission.

Would You Rather? Sample questions

1. Would you rather always wear earmuffs or a nose plug?
2. Would you rather be a deep sea diver or an astronaut?
3. Would you rather be a dog named Killer or a cat named Fluffy?
4. Would you rather be a giant mouse or a tiny dinosaur?
5. Would you rather be able to hear any conversation or take back anything you say?
6. Would you rather be able to read everyone's mind all the time or always know their future?
7. Would you rather be able to stop time or fly?
8. Would you rather be an unknown minor league basketball player or a famous professional badminton star?
9. Would you rather be born with an elephant trunk or a giraffe neck?
10. Would you rather drink a cup of olive oil or a cup of pickle juice.

Grocery List—Sample

Pantry/cupboards:		**Refrigerator:**		**Bathroom:**	
	Soup		Milk		Soap
	Syrup – Pancake		Butter		Shampoo & Conditioner
	Rice		Cheese		Mouth Wash
	Sugar – White		Lunch Meat		Toothpaste
	Tortilla Chips		Ketchup		Floss
	Bars – Granola Type		Mayo		Q Tips
	Honey		Jam – Strawberry	**Oops, I forgot:**	
	Coffee		Eggs		
	Cereal		Bread		
	Cinnamon	**Freezer:**			
	Salt		Hamburger Patties		
	Pepper		Ice Cream		
Produce:			Waffles – Frozen		
	Oranges		Pizza		
	Apples	**Household:**			
	Bananas		Dishwasher Detergent		
	Lettuce		Dish Soap	**Notes for next time:**	
	Tomatoes		Paper Plates		
			Napkins		
			Garbage Bags		
			Toilet Paper		

Social Autopsy Worksheet

When needed, sit down with the child and help them fill out this worksheet to help them understand how their behavior affected a social situation. Either you or the child can draw or write each step below.

Here's what was going on:	Here's what I did that caused a social error:	Here's what happened when I did that:	Here's what I should do to make things right:	Here's what I'll do next time:

Adapted from the work of Rick Lavoie (2005).

The Six Sides of Breathing

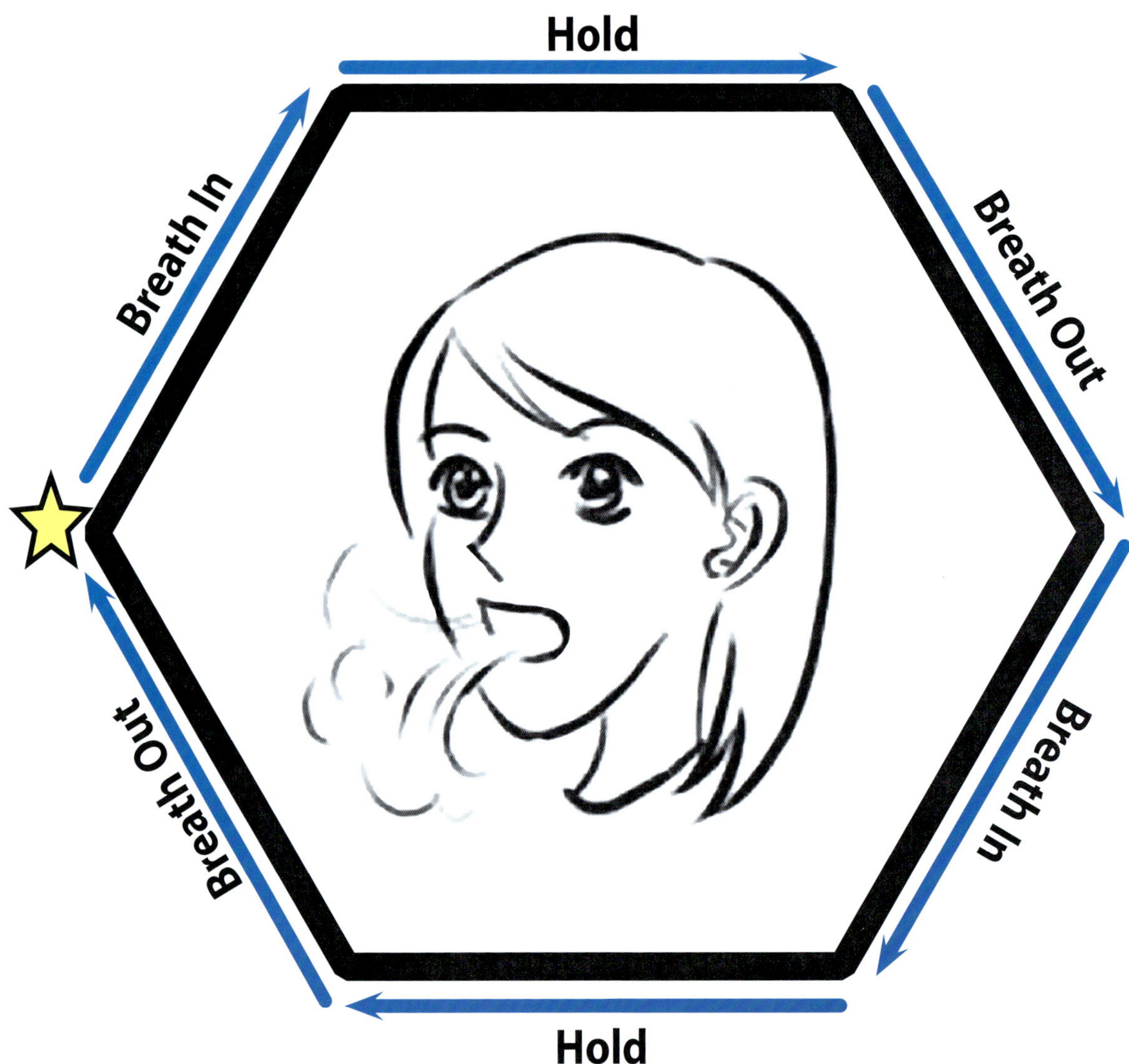

Starting at the yellow star trace with your finger the sides of the hexagon as you take a deep breath in, feeling your shoulders rise as the air fills you. Trace over the next side as you hold your breath for a moment. Slowly breathe out as you trace the third side of the hexagon. Continue tracing around the bottom three sides of the hexagon as you complete another deep breath. Continue The Six Sides of Breathing cycle until you feel calm and relaxed.

From L. Kuypers, *The Zones of Regulation*, 2008, San Jose, CA: Social Thinking Publishing, p. 118. Used with permission.

Kid Tricks—Sample

Teach the child simple and fun skills to build confidence and use to break the ice when meeting new people or connecting with old ones. Below are some silly ideas to get started. Most will require demonstration and lots of practice. Once the child becomes a pro, encourage him or her to teach the skill to others.

Shuffling Cards – Split the deck of cards in half and hold half in each hand. Put your thumb on the edge of the cards that you want to merge into the other half of the deck. Put your ring and middle finger on the other end of the cards. Arch the cards in each hand and slowly pull your thumbs back, which will release the cards and file them into each other. With half of the deck merged into the other half, hold the position of your hands and bend the cards the other way so that they shuffle into each other and form a flat deck of cards.

Blowing Bubbles – Chew gum until it is soft. Make the gum flat and put it between the top of your mouth and the tongue. Hold the flattened gum with your jaw and stick your tongue slightly against the gum while blowing at the same time. Continue to blow until it is large enough to stop or it pops.

Skipping a Stone – Find a calm body of water and a flat, small stone. Hold the stone with your thumb and middle finger on either side of the edges, keeping the flat part up. Stand facing the water or to the side so that your body can twist toward the water then you throw. Aim and throw the stone very hard across the surface of the water with the flat part of the stone face up. Watch the stone dance and skip on the top of the water.

Doing Cartwheels – Make sure you have plenty of room and a flat, soft, safe space. Look for a straight line and spread your feet apart and put your arms straight above your head with your palms facing out and elbows straight. Turn one foot in the direction you want to go and bend over sideways while kicking your legs off the ground and into the air. Keep your eyes looking at your hands and where your feet will land and place your feet firmly on the ground. It should go hand, hand, foot, foot in that order on the ground.

Juggling – Get three beanbags or balls that do not bounce. Practice passing one ball from one hand to the other and throwing one ball in the air and catching it with the same hand. Practice "scooping," which is a simple shallow scoop or dip that you do with your hand before tossing the ball in the air. Practice tossing with two balls, throwing them in the air and catching them. When the first ball is at the peak of the arc, toss the next one, catching them as they fall. When comfortable with this, add a third ball. Throw the balls in the air when they are at the peak of the arc, always ready with another ball to throw up.

Jokes – Get a joke book or go online to look up age appropriate jokes. Make sure you pick a joke that is appropriate for the audience, especially for the age and the interest of the people you are telling it to. If you tell a joke that is topic specific or that is too complicated for the age of the listener, it won't be funny. Practice the joke by yourself or with a family member. Practice setting it up (laying the foundation) and making a strong punchline (the funny part). If the listener doesn't get it or think it's funny, try to explain it so they join in the laughter/humor.

Fun With Language – Teach your child a made up language such as Pig Latin, a code language, or even a tongue twister that they can teach to other children such as "She sells seashells on the seashore".

Whistling – Shape the lips as if you were going to make the sound "ooh" or in a small circle (e.g., pucker lips). Curl the tongue slightly on each edge and press it against the roof of the mouth. Blow a steady, smooth stream of air through the opening of the tongue and lips. Adjust lips and tongue position until sound comes out as a whistling noise.

Funny Facts – Have your child research funny, interesting, or odd facts to share with others, such as "It's impossible to sneeze with your eyes open" or "Rabbits and parrots can see behind themselves without even moving their heads!". They can practice telling these to the family first and then branch out to their peers when ready. Help them use phrases such as "did you know?"... or "I just learned something interesting, do you want to know, too?"

Special Interests and Knowledge – For kids who have a special interest such as geography, trains, number knowledge or sports information, have them practice sharing that information with their peers in a way that makes other people interested. For example, if they know a lot about geography or sports, they can have a peer quiz them about state capitals or which sports teams play in different states.

Social Narrative—Sample

Use this or a similar story to help the child know what is going to happen when going to the beach.

This vacation I will be spending time at the beach. I will bring towels and chairs to sit on and food to eat. It is usually sunny at the beach, so I will need my sunglasses and sunscreen.

I will play in the sand and in the water. If there are other kids playing in the sand or water, I can ask them to play with me. Maybe we can build a sand castle together. I will share my sand toys with the other kids.

I will try not to get sand on other people when they are lying on their towels or in the food. I will be careful when I am in the ocean and stay with an adult at all times when I am in the water. The sand might be hot, and the ocean might be cold.

Going to the beach is fun and relaxing.

Interest Inventory/Reinforcement Menu

Ask the child to put a check next to at least five items/activities that he or she would most like to earn at home. Add items or change the list to make it specific for the child. (Read the list to non-readers or use photos or visuals and help them mark the items they select.)

_____1. Hug, high five, or verbal praise

_____2. Food treat (can be specific here)

_____3. Coloring/drawing

_____4. Computer time, video games, TV

_____5. Play with friends

_____6. Stickers

_____7. Going for a walk

_____8. Play with favorite toy (can be specific; Legos®, puzzles, train, Barbies®)

_____9. Reading time

_____10. Time with adult

_____11. Written note about good behavior on refrigerator

Setting Up Successful Play Dates

- Make sure the child is ready and willing to have a play date. Don't force anything or put the child in a situation that is too challenging, such as going swimming if the child does not know how to swim. It is important to make sure it is a successful and rewarding experience for everybody involved.
- Start at a park or neutral place. Sometimes just hanging out on the playground after school is a great start. It can be hard for some kids to understand what having a guest means and how to share or welcome a guest. Have a play date at your home before sending the child to a friend's house.
- Keep it short and limit the amount of children at one given time.
- Pick a good time. Make sure the child is well rested, healthy, and that the date is absent of new transitions and/or changes. Avoid nap times, difficult times in the day for the child, periods after a holiday or vacation when schedules/routines have changed.
- Pick well-matched play partners—this significantly influences the process. Generally, select children who are younger or a little older, or familiar kids that the child prefers. Do not include siblings at first because the playmate/guest might prefer playing with the sibling.
- Try to schedule play dates on a regular basis—at a park, another person's house or your house for an after-school snack.
- Plan ahead. Arrange for preferred, familiar games or activities (e.g., art, hide-and-seek, duck, duck goose). Sharing and trading can be hard at first, so prepare the child by talking to him about what a guest is and what is *expected* of both the host and the guest. Talk about the rules with both of the children at the start of the play date. Remove special toys and have two toys for each activity.
- Get involved. Don't just let them play by themselves and hope for the best. Change activities when needed, help with sharing and negotiating and facilitating play together, but don't dominate or fill in for the child. The idea is to break the ice, reinforce, and facilitate without taking control. Back off as soon as you can.
- Make the last 15 minutes the most fun (e.g., snack or special activity) as this is what the children will remember best. Recap the play date and discuss what went well and what didn't.
- Be a play date yourself. This is a good way to figure out what areas the child needs help in and to identify her strengths (if she struggles with puzzles, leave them out of play dates with kids, etc.). Don't forget to model *expected* social behavior yourself—imitation is HUGE! Narrate your feelings, thoughts, and actions.
- If the child isn't ready for other children, a furry friend or pet can be less threatening and a good introduction to being social. For example, have the child play with the dog by throwing a ball to him. This back-and-forth interaction can be a start to interacting more with other people.
- Don't expect too much too early. If the child is younger, it is developmentally appropriate to play mostly side-by-side and imitate rather than interact. Too much pressure can cause stress on both the child and the play date.

Sample Intentions of the Day

"I will do my best."

"I will give it a try."

"It's nice to be nice."

"Doing my best is the best I can do."

"I believe in me."

"I will look for the good in others."

"I will focus on the good things today."

"Mistakes are how I grow and learn."

"It's okay to make mistakes."

"I am enough."

"Today, I am grateful for ____"

"It's okay to not know everything."

List of Sensation Words

This list will help you model and teach the awareness of sensation words to build vocabulary for your child to describe how they are feeling in their body.

achy	damp	heavy	relaxed	sweaty
awake	dark	hot	sensitive	tender
breathless	dense	icy	shaky	tense
brittle	dizzy	itchy	shivery	thick
bruised	empty	jittery	smooth	thin
bubbly	energized	jumpy	soft	throbbing
burning	expansive	knotted	sore	tingly
buzzy	explosive	light	spacey	tight
calm	fiery	melting	spacious	trembly
clammy	floating	nauseous	spinning	twitchy
clenched	fluttery	numb	still	warm
cold	frantic	piercing	stretchy	weighted
congested	frozen	pounding	strong	wet
cool	full	prickly	stuck	
cozy	fuzzy	pulsing	stuffy	

Body Scan

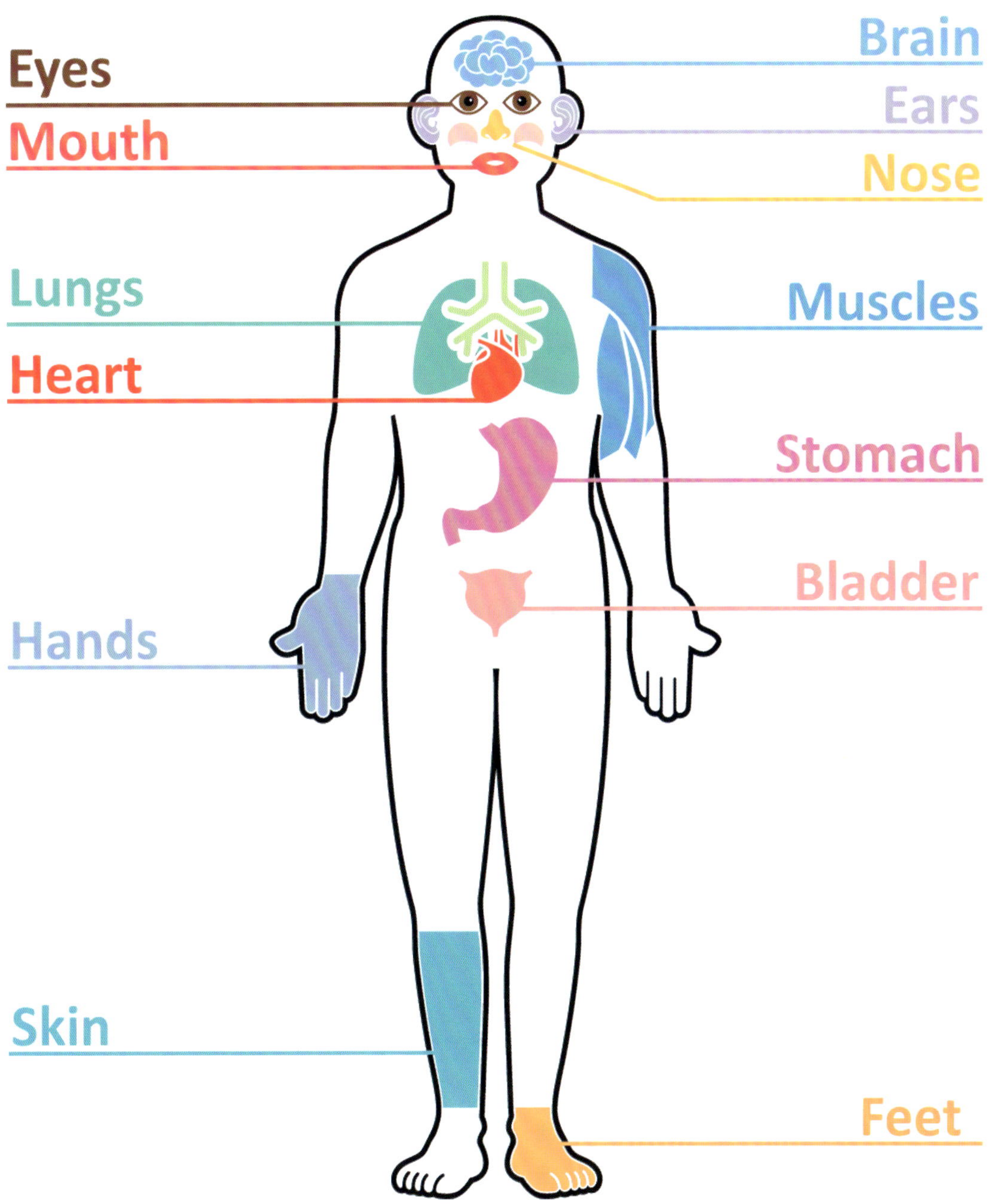

Reprinted with permission from *The Interoception Curriculum: A Step-by-Step Framework for Developing Mindful Self-Regulation* (Mahler, 2019)

Chores By Age

When getting children involved in doing chores, it is important to keep in mind their age and abilities.

2–3 YEARS OLD

- Pick up toys
- Put dirty clothes in the laundry
- Help put away groceries
- Help unload the dishwasher
- Help dust
- Feed pet(s)
- Clear place after meals
- Help clean up their own messes (spills, etc)
- Pull weeds
- Help set the table
- Assist in making the bed
- Put clean clothes in drawer
- Water plants

4–5 YEARS OLD

- All previous chores
- Make their bed
- Put away laundry
- Throw away trash
- Make a snack
- Get a drink by themselves
- Put dirty dishes in the dishwasher
- Help cook dinner
- Help wipe off table tops
- Fold towels and washcloths
- Help clean their bedroom
- Bring mail into the house
- Replace bathroom towels

6–8 YEARS OLD

- All previous chores
- Help pack school lunch
- Sweep floors
- Mop floors
- Get trash from the bathrooms and bedrooms
- Help organize closets and drawers
- Rake leaves
- Clean mirrors/windows
- Clean counters
- Get themselves up in the morning with an alarm clock

9–11 YEARS OLD

- All previous chores
- Clean up after pets
- Ironing own clothes
- Change lightbulbs, replace appliance batteries
- Clean refrigerator, showers, toilets
- Wash car
- Vacuum inside of car
- Gather trash and take the dumpster to the curb
- Operate the dishwasher
- Cook a complete meal

12+ YEARS OLD

- All previous chores
- Mow the lawn
- Sort clothes that no longer fit
- Supervise younger siblings
- Help paint
- Help with grocery
- Shopping
- Laundry start to finish
- Meal plan
- Clean bathroom
- Take out neighbor's garbage

List of Emotion/Feeling Words

Use this list of emotion words to refer to when talking to your child about how you feel and also to teach new emotional vocabulary.

Consider selecting an emotion "word of the week" to be aware of and learn about.

afraid
angry
anxious
blue
bored
brave
calm cautious
cheerful
confused
content

crabby
curious
defeated
delighted
depressed
disappointed
disgusted
disturbed
eager
embarrassed
excited

fantastic
fascinated
friendly
furious
generous
gloomy
grateful
grouchy
homesick
hopeless
hurt

impatient
interested
jealous
lonely
loving
nervous
overwhelmed
peaceful
proud
relieved
satisfied

scared
shy
silly
shocked
stubborn
stunned
surprised
tense
uncomfortable
upbeat
worried

Sample Letter to Teacher

Welcome to "Team X (Child's Name)"
(Date)
CONFIDENTIAL; NOT FOR DISTRIBUTION

Hello Mr. Smith. We are excited that Sarah will be in your class this year and wanted to provide some background information here that might be helpful to you and others who will be on the team.

Parent's Contact: Elaine Watson
(555)555-5555

Other relative or people in charge: Susan Rumsey (Aunt)
(555)555-0000

Facts:

Date of Birth: 06/07/2013
Grade: 1st
Allergies: peanuts
Blood Type: O+
Medications: Setraline

TRIGGERS/STRESSORS:

Loud noises
Transitions
Strong smells
Being tired
Being bored

TIPS/STRATEGIES:

Use noise-cancelling headphones.
Prepare for transitions.
Let her take breaks.
Make sure she has work at her level.

IF TRIGGERED/DYSREGULATED:

Have her talk to an adult, validate feelings, take a break, listen to music, read, or write in her journal.

DIAGNOSES:

ASD

SENSORY-SEEKING/REGULATING BEHAVIORS:

Spinning
Jumping on a trampoline
Jumping Jacks
Wall Sit-ups

INTERVENTIONS:

Social skills group outside of school

HELPFUL RESOURCES/OTHER INFORMATION:

Zones of Regulation, social stories

GOALS:

Join in social situations.
Start/Initiate conversations.
Advocate when she needs support.

Priming Your Child For A Social Event/Outing

Fill this out prior to the event and review a few times with your child. Add pictures of the place, people, or other visuals that might help prepare and set your child up for success.

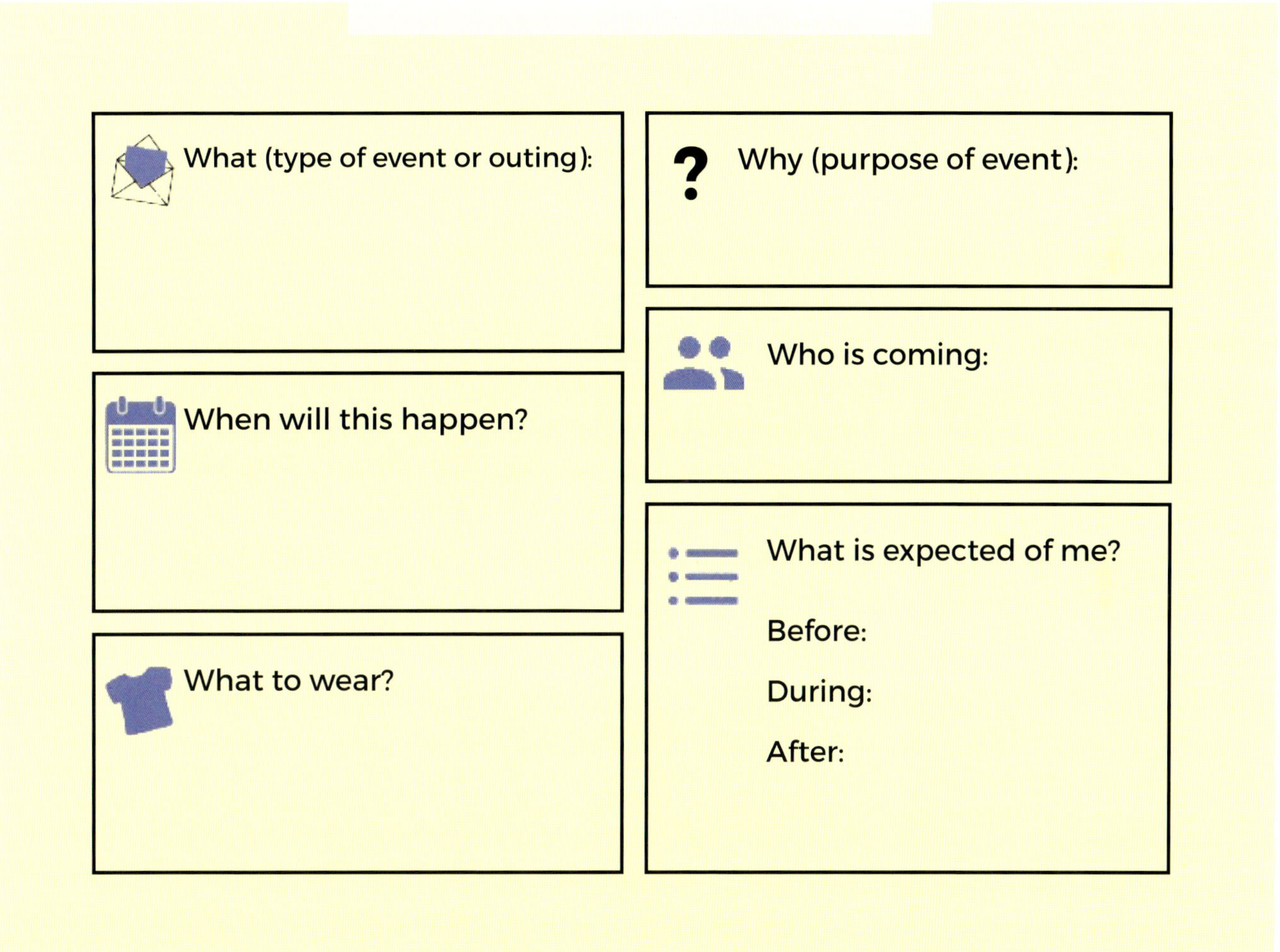

Suggested Extracurricular Activities

Physical/Sports Interests

Sports and board games are not just about winning and losing. Although those are important skills to learn to manage gracefully, children learn many other skills through play, such as problem solving, negotiating, turn-taking, conflict resolution, patience, sportsmanship, how to follow the rules, and how to relate to others. Below are some suggestions for games and sports the child might enjoy. Always keep the child's interests and skills in mind. If you opt for a team sport, investigate the coach's style and expectations before getting the child involved. Have the child watch someone else playing the game or sport to build interest, awareness, and confidence before jumping in.

To start, consider sports/recreational activities that don't create excessive pressure to perform for the team, including

- Swimming
- Karate
- Tennis
- Skiing

When ready, choose sports that involve practicing teamwork and sportsmanship, including

- Swim team
- Track and field
- Soccer
- Baseball
- Basketball

Academic Interests

For children who are more academically driven or have an artistic/creative side, use these interests and skills to help incorporate social participation. Academic group work and study groups can bring children together to practice social interaction. Clubs, events, or activities that include others are great ways to get involved and practice working with others.

- Chess
- Book club
- Science club
- Computer club
- Debate team
- Journalism

Creative Interests

- Art
- Pottery
- Drama
- Music/band
- Puzzles with other people
- Wii® sports with others
- Boy/Girl Scouts
- Building Legos® or other construction

Other

- Card games that involve other people (not solitaire)
- Pokémon® or other trading cards with friends
- Board games

Note about special interests (trains, Legos®, Star Wars®, bugs, etc.): Try to find a way to incorporate the child's special interests into a social event. For example, have the child build a model train with another student in an art class or on a play date.

Recommended Movies

- *Playtime With Zeebu* (Thought Bubble Productions)
- *Wallace and Gromit* (National Film and Television School, Aardman Animations, DreamWorks, DreamWorks Animation)
- *The Pink Panther*, rated PG (Sony Pictures Home Entertainment)
- *Charlie Brown* movies or TV specials by Charles Schultz
- *Finding Nemo*, rated G (Walt Disney Studios Home Entertainment 2003)
- *Toy Story*, rated G (Pixar Animation Studios)
- *Bean* and *Mr. Bean's Holiday*, rated PG 13 (Working Title Films)
- Claymation movies – many titles and companies
- *Winnie the Pooh* movies, rated G (Disney)

Recommended Games

The following are examples of games for improving all areas of language, including social skills. Playing games with the child also helps with turn taking, sharing, flexibility, problem solving, and sportsmanship. Games can be modified depending on the child's needs. Start slowly with just you and the child. Model and reinforce positive social interactions and skills. When the child is comfortable playing with you, begin to add siblings or other children to practice what the child has learned.

Board and Card Games

- *Apples to Apples®* – Mattel
- *Battleship®* – Milton Bradley
- *Blurt®* – made by Blurt
- *Bubble Brain®* – Patch Products
- *Cranium Cadoo®* – Cranium, Inc.
- *Cranium Whoonu®* – Cranium, Inc.
- *Emotional Bingo®* – Active Parenting Publishers
- *Go Fish®* and *Kings®* (card games)
- *Guess Where®* – Hasbro, Milton Bradley and others
- *Guess Who®* – Hasbro, Milton Bradley and others
- *Guesstures®* – Milton Bradley
- *Hedbanz®* – Spin Master Games
- *I Spy Preschool Game®* – Briarpatch
- *Kids on Stage®* – Kids on Stage, Inc.
- *Mad Chatter®* – Hersch & Co.
- *Mad Libs®* – Price, Stern, Sloan
- *Outburst Junior®* – Parker Brothers
- *Pictionary and Pictionary Jr.®* – Hasbro
- *Red Light, Green Light®* – Tara Toy Corp.
- *Scattergories®* – Hasbro
- *Should I or Should I Not®* – Social Thinking
- *Taboo and Taboo Junior®* – Hasbro
- *Twister®* – Milton Bradley
- *Would You Rather?®* – Zobmondo
- *You Gotta Be Kidding®* – Zobmondo

Other Family Games

- Charades
- Follow the leader
- Freeze dance
- Hide and seek
- Musical chairs
- Scavenger hunts
- "Simon Says ..."

References and Recommended Reading

Atwood, T. (1998). *Asperger's syndrome: A guide for parents and professionals*. Philadelphia, PA: Jessica Kingsley Publishers Limited (USA).

Ayres, A. J. (2005). *Sensory integration and the child*. Los Angeles, CA: Western Psychological Services.

Baron-Cohen, S. (1995). *Mindblindness: An essay on autism and theory of mind*. Cambridge, MA: The MIT Press.

Baron-Cohen, S., Leslie, A., & Frith, U. (1985). Does the autistic child have a"theory of mind"? *Cognition, 21*, 37-46.

Barry, T. D., Klingler, L. G., Lee, J. M., Palardy, N., Gilmore, T., & Bodin, S. D. (2003). Examining the effectiveness of an outpatient clinic social skills group for high-functioning children with autism. *Journal of Autism and Developmental Disorders*, *33*(6), 685-701.

Bodrova, E., & Leong, D. J. (2005). Self-regulation as a key to school readiness: How can early childhood teachers promote this critical competence? In M. Zaslow & I. Martinez-Beck (Eds.), *Critical issues in early childhood professional development* (section III). Baltimore, MD: Paul H. Brookes Publishing.

Bodrova, E., & Leong, D. J. (2007). *Tools of the mind: The Vygotskian approach to early childhood education* (2nd ed.). New York: Prentice-Hall.

Bogen Novak, H. & Lindemuth, C. (2015). *The Brain Talk Curriculum*. Oakland, CA: Brain Learning and Metacognitive Thinking Curriculum.

Bolick, T. (2001). *Asperger Syndrome and adolescence: Helping preteens and teens get ready for the real world*. Gloucester, MA: Fair Winds Press.

Branstetter, R. (2013). The Everything Parent's Guide to Children with Executive Functioning Disorder: Strategies to help your child achieve the time-management skills, focus, and organization needed to succeed in school and life. Avon, MA: Adams Media.

Branstetter, R. (2015) The Conscious Parent's Guide To ADHD: A Mindful Approach for Helping Your Child Gain Focus and Self-Control. Avon, MA: Adams Media.

Bryan, C. J., Dweck, C. S., Rogers, T., & Walton, M. (2011). Motivating voter turnout by motivating the self. *Proceedings of the National Academy of Sciences, 108*(31), 12653-12656.

Buron, K. D., & Curtis, M. (2012). *The incredible 5-point scale.* Shawnee Mission, KS: AAPC Publishing.

Buron, K., & Wolfberg, P. (2008). *Learners on the autism spectrum, preparing highly qualified educators*. Shawnee Mission, KS: AAPC Publishing.

Buron, K., & Wolfberg, P. (2014). *Learners on the autism spectrum, preparing highly qualified educators* (2nd ed.). Shawnee Mission, KS: AAPC Publishing.

Cox, A. J. (2007). *No mind left behind: Understanding and fostering executive control- the eight essential brain skills every child needs to thrive.* New York, NY: Penguin Group (USA), Inc.

Dawson, P., & Guare, R. (2010). *Executive skills in children & adolescents* (2nd ed.). New York, NY: Guilford Publications.

Dweck, C. (2006). *Mindset*. New York, NY: Random House.

Faber, A., & Mazlish, E. (1980). *How to talk so kids will listen and listen so kids will talk.* New York, NY: Rawson, Wade Publishers, Inc.

Faber, J. and King, J., (2017). *How To Talk So LITTLE Kids Will Listen: A Survival Guide to Life with Children Ages 2-7*/ Scribner, NY. Companion app: *Pocket Parent* (Mythic Owl).

Gillespie, L., & Seibel, N. (2006). Self-regulation: A cornerstone of early childhood development. *Beyond the Journal: Young Children on the Web*. Retrieved from http://journal.naeyc.org/btj/200607/Gillespie709BTJ.pdf

Goldstein, H., Kaczmarek, L. A., & English, K. M. (2002). *Promoting social communication: Children with developmental disabilities from birth to adolescence*. Baltimore, MD: Paul H. Brookes Publishing Co.

Goleman, D. (1995). *Emotional intelligence: Why it can matter more than IQ* (10th anniversary ed.). New York, NY: Bantam, Random House, Inc.

Grau, V., & Whitebread, D. (2012). Self and social regulation of learning during collaborative activities in the classroom: The interplay of individual and group cognition. *Learning and Instruction, 22*(6), 401-412.

Gray, C. (2000). *The new Social StoryTM book*. Arlington, TX: Future Horizons, Inc. Greene, R. (1999). *The explosive child*. New York, NY: HarperCollins.

Greenspan, S. L., Wieder, S. , & Simons, R. (2008). *The child with special needs: Encouraging intellectual and emotional growth*. Reading, MA: Addison-Wesley.

Gruber, R., Cassoff, J., Frenette, S., Wiebe, S., & Carrier, J. (2012). The impact of sleep extension and restriction on children's emotional liability and impulsivity. *Pediatrics*, *130* (5), e1155-e1161. doi: 10.1542/peds.2012-0564

Halloran, J. (2018). *Coping Skills for Kids Workbook: Over 75 Coping Strategies to Help Kids Deal with Stress, Anxiety and Anger*. Eau Claire, WI: PESI Publishing & Media.

Harrison, T., & Watkins, M. (2020). *The Brain's Playground: Using Improv Games To Teach Social and Emotional Learning*. Pleasant Hill, CA: Partington Behavior Analysts

Heyman, G. (2008). Talking about success: Implications for achievement motivation. *Journal of Applied Developmental Psychology, 29*(5), 361-370.

Jacobsen P. (2005). *Understanding how Asperger children and adolescents think and learn*. London, UK, and Philadelphia, PA: Jessica Kingsley Publishers.

Koegel, L. K., Koegel, R. L., Frea, W., & Green-Hopkins, I. (2003). Priming as a method of coordinating educational services for students with autism. *Language, Speech, and Hearing Services in Schools, 34,* 228-235.

Koegel, L., Matos-Fredeen, R., Lang, R., & Koegel, R. (2011). Interventions for children with autism spectrum disorders in inclusive school settings. *Cognitive and Behavioral Practice,* CBPRA-00350. doi:10.1016/j.cbpra.2010.11.003

Kuypers, L. M. (2008). *The zones of regulation*. San Jose, CA: Social Thinking Publishing.

Kuypers, L., & Sautter, E. (2012, May-June). How to promote social regulation. *Autism Bay Area Magazine*, pp. 8-9.

Lantieri, L. (2008). *Building emotional intelligence: Techniques to cultivate inner strength in children*. Boulder, CO: Sounds True, Inc.

Levine, M. (2012). *Teach your children well: Parenting for authentic success*. New York, NY: HarperCollins.

Lavoie, R. (2005). *It's so much work to be your friend: Helping the child with learning disabilities find social success*. New York, NY: Simon & Schuster.

Lavoie, R. (2005). Social skill autopsies: A strategy to promote and develop social competencies. *LDonline*. Retrieved from http://www.ldonline.org/ article/14910/

MacDuff, G., Krantz, P., & McClannahan, L. (2001). Prompts and prompt-fading strategies for people with autism. In C. Maurice, G. Green, & R. M. Foxx *(Eds.), Making a difference: Behavioral intervention for autism* (pp. 37-50). Austin, TX: Pro-Ed.

Madrigal, S., & Winner, M. G. (2008). *Superflex: A superhero social thinking curriculum*. San Jose, CA: Social Thinking Publishing.

Mahler, K. (2016). *Interoception: The eighth sensory system: Practical Solutions for improving self-regulation, self-awareness and social understanding of individuals with autism spectrum and related disorders*. Shawnee Mission, KS: AAPC

Mahler, K. (2019). *The Interoception Curriculum: A Step-by-Step Guide to Developing Mindful Self-Regulation*. Lancaster, PA: Mahler

Maurice, C., Green, G., & Luce, S. C. (Eds.). (1996). *Behavioral intervention for young children with autism: A manual for parents and professionals*. Austin, TX: Pro-Ed, Inc.

McAfee, J. (2002). *Navigating the social world*. Arlington, TX: Future Horizons, Inc.

McClelland, M. M., Ponitz, C. C., Messersmith, E. E., & Tominey, S. (2010). Self-regulation: The integration of cognition and emotion. In R. Lerner (Series Ed.) & W. Overton (Vol. Ed.), *Handbook of lifespan human development, Vol. 4. Cognition, biology, and methods* (pp. 509–553). Hoboken, NJ: Wiley.

McCurry, C. (2009). *Parenting your anxious child with mindfulness and acceptance: A powerful new approach to overcoming fear, panic, and worry using acceptance and commitment therapy*. Oakland, CA: New Harbinger Publications, Inc.

Miller, C. (2006). Developmental relationships between language and theory of mind. *American Journal of Speech-Language Pathology*, *15*, 142-154.

Myles, B. S., Trautman, M. L. , & Schelvan, R. L. (2013). *The hidden curriculum for understanding unstated rules in social situations for adolescents and young adults* (2nd ed.). Shawnee Mission, KS: AAPC Publishing.

Myles, J. M., & Kolar, A. (2013). *The hidden curriculum and other everyday challenges for elementary-age children with high-functioning autism*. Shawnee Mission, KS: AAPC Publishing.

National Autism Center. (2011). *A parent's guide to evidence-based practice and autism*. Retrieved from http://www.nationalautismcenter.org/learning/ parent_manual.php

Ozonoff, S., Dawson, J., & McPartland, J. (2002). *A parent's guide to Asperger syndrome and high-functioning autism.* New York, NY: The Guilford Press.

Patrick, H. (1997). Social self-regulation: Exploring the relations between children's social relationships, academic self-regulation, and school performance. *Educational Psychologist, 32*(4), 209-220.

Peters, D.B. (2013). *Make Your Warrior a Warrior: A Guide to Conquering Your Child's Fears.* Scottsdale, AZ: Great Potential Press.

Peters, D.B. (2013). *From Warrior to Warrior: A Guide to Conquering Your Fears.* Scottsdale, AZ: Great Potential Press.

Prizant, B., Wetherby, A., Rubin, E., Laurent, A., & Rydell, P. (2006). *The SCERTS® model: A comprehensive educational approach for children with autism spectrum disorders* . Baltimore, MD: Brookes Publishing.

Rapee, R., Wignall, A., Spence, S., Cobham, V., & Lyneham, H. (2000). *Helping your anxious child.* Oakland, CA: New Harbinger Publications, Inc.

Reber, Deborah (2018). *Differently Wired: Raising an Exceptional Child in a Conventional World.* New York: Workman Publishing.

Roberts, M., & Kaiser, A. (2011). The Effectiveness of Parent-Implemented Language Intervention: A Meta-Analysis. *American Journal of Speech-Language Pathology, 20*, 180-199.

Sautter, E., & Wilson, K. (2011). *Whole body listening Larry at home.* San Jose, CA: Social Thinking Publishing.

Sautter, E., & Wilson, K. (2011). *Whole body listening Larry at school.* San Jose, CA: Social Thinking Publishing.

Shonkoff, J., & Phillips, D. (2000). *From neurons to neighborhoods: The science of early childhood development.* Washington, DC: National Academies Press.

Siegel, D. I., & Bryson T. (2011). *The whole-brain child: 12 revolutionary strategies to nurture your child's developing mind, survive everyday parenting struggles, and help your family thrive.* New York, NY: The Random House Publishing Company.

Siegel, D. J., & Bryson, T. P. (2019). *The yes brain: How to cultivate courage, curiosity, and resilience in your child.* New York, NY: Bantam.

Siegel, D. J., & Bryson, T. P. (2020). *The power of showing up: How parental presence shapes who our kids become and how their brains get wired.* New York, NY: Ballantine Books.

Sohn, A., & Grayson, C. (2005). *Parenting your Asperger child: Individualized solutions for teaching the child practical skills.* New York, NY: Penguin Group (USA), Inc.

Stewart, K. K., Carr, J. E., & LeBlanc, L. A. (2007). Evaluation of family-implemented behavioral skills training for teaching social skills to a child with Asperger's Disorder. *Clinical Case Studies, 6*(3), 252-262.

Taylor-Klaus, E. (2020). *The Essential Guide to Raising Complex Kids with ADHD, Anxiety, and More.* Beverly, MA: Fair Winds Press, an imprint of The Quarto Group

Townsend J, & Rubin E. (2018) Social Emotional Engagement - Knowledge and Skills (SEE-KS) for 2018 UDL-IRN Summit Proceedings. Retrieved from: https://udl-irn.org/wp-content/uploads/2018/04/Done_TOWNSEND.EDIT_.DH_.JEG_.pdf.

Truesdale, S. P. (1990). Whole body listening: Developing active auditory skills. *Language, Speech, and Hearing Services in Schools, 23*, 183-184.

Vagin, A. (2012). *Movie time social learning.* San Jose, CA: Social Thinking Publishing.

Vermeulen, P. (2013). *Autism as context blindness* (textbook ed.). Shawnee Mission, KS: AAPC Publishing.

Volet, S., Vauras, M., & Salonen, P. (2009). Self- and social regulation in learning contexts: An integrative perspective. *Educational Psychologist, 44*(4), 215-226.

Ward, S. (2013). *Practical strategies to improve executive function skills.* Presentation at Communication Works and the annual Social Thinking Provider's Conference, San Francisco, CA.

Ward, S., & Jacobsen, K. (2012). *Cognitive connections*. Concord, MA: Executive Function Practice.

Winner, M.G. (2007) Thinking About You Thinking About Me. Think Social Publishing, Inc.

Winner, M.G. and Murphy, L. (2016). Social Thinking and Me. Think Social Publishing, Inc.

Wolfberg, P. (2003). *Peer play and the autism spectrum: The art of guiding children's socialization and imagination.* Shawnee Mission, KS: AAPC Publishing.

Wolfberg, P. J. (2009). *Play and imagination in children with autism* (2nd ed.). New York, NY: Columbia, Teachers College Press.

Kabat-Zinn, J. (2015). Mindfulness. *Mindfulness, 6*(6).

Gratitude

Who knew that writing a book (even for the second time) would be such a consuming and invigorating experience. I couldn't have done it without a support team.

I am deeply grateful for all of the brilliant therapists, coworkers, parents/caregivers, and courageous children, teens, and adults at Communication Works (CW) with whom I have worked over the years and learned so much from. A special shout out to Hillary, Audra, Anthony, Megan, May, and Sally for making our work-family run so smoothly! I love helping others "Communicate and Connect" alongside all of you!

Thank you Anna, Carrie, Eliza, Emily, Katie, Lauren, Leah, Rae, Rebecca, Monica, and Terri for geeking out with me on my favorite thing to talk about—social-emotional learning—and agreeing with me that there is nothing more important in life.

To my amazing book production team and editors: Bekah, Chris, Cindy, Debbie, Erin, Gretchen, James, Katie, Kristen, Linda, McKenna, Rachel, Rae, Ruby, Ruth and Saumya. Thanks for holding my hand; I couldn't have done this without you!

Thank you Mom, Dad, Karlene, Joel, and the rest of my family (and extended friend-family) for listening to and loving me.

To my partner, Anthony: thanks for dealing with me through everything. You are the best husband, father, co-worker, and friend! To my two energetic, sweet boys, Julian and Gabriel, who keep me on my toes and remind me that being a parent is not easy, but is the most important job in the world. I love you dearly and thank you for forgiving me for not being the perfect mom.

A big thank you to Emily, Kari, Kelly, Leah, Michelle, Pamela, Rebecca, Ruth, and Sarah (see bios on page i-ii) for your contributions, inspiration, and expertise in the field. I have learned so much from your work and appreciate you sharing it with my readers.

I am grateful!

About the Author

Elizabeth Sautter, M.A., CCC, is a speech and language pathologist, award-winning author, blogger, and highly sought-after speaker specializing in social and emotional learning since 1996. Elizabeth's interest in social learning began early while growing up with a sister with developmental challenges. She is also a mom of two teens with complex social, emotional, and academic needs. These personal experiences have fueled a passion in her to serve individuals and their families who are struggling with everyday challenges.

Elizabeth is the creator of *MakeSocialLearningStick.com*, which provides consultation, training (including the *Make it Stick* online parenting course), and resources to assist children, teens, and their families in building skills and practical strategies to manage emotions, navigate social situations, and achieve their goals. She is the co-author of the popular children's book series *Whole Body Listening Larry*. She is a collaborative trainer for the Zones of Regulation and co-author of the accompanying storybooks, card decks, and games.

Elizabeth is the co-founder of Communication Works, a speech therapy practice providing services to schools, individuals, and their families. She lives in the Bay Area with her husband, two teenage sons, a cat, and a dog. She firmly believes that social-emotional learning has changed her life and wants to share those skills with others.

MakeSocialLearningStick.com